THE

LOST
SAN SABA MINES

By C. F. Eckhardt

Texas
Monthly
Press

Texas Monthly Press, Inc.
P.O. Box 1569
Austin, Texas 78767

A B C D E F G.H

Library of Congress Cataloging in Publication Data

Eckhardt, C. F.
  The lost San Saba mines.

  1.Mines and mineral resources—Texas—History.
I. Title
TN24.T4E23   338.2'7421'0976462   82-5677
ISBN 0-932012-34-5   AACR2

Text Design and Production by the Composing Stick
Illustrations by Suzanne Pustejovsky

CONTENTS
The Lost San Saba Mines

v

To Ralph A. Doyal, who should have been a legend, but was born a few years too late. The grass is tall and the water sweet, so they say, where you ride now, old friend. Is there silver in those hills, too?

Acknowledgments

A book is never written by one person alone. Literally hundreds of people helped in one way or another in the writing of this one. First and foremost, there was my friend, Ralph A. Doyal. J. Frank Dobie wrote the books that got me started, and my mother, Evelyn Eckhardt, gave them to me. My long-suffering wife, Vicki W. Eckhardt, endured the rattling typewriter and the inevitable chaos that is the usual condition of the household of those who have books in gestation. William Edward Syers opened a lot of doors that might otherwise have stayed shut and at the same time gave a much needed shove. Mrs. J. Morton Hardison and her daughter, Peggy Liggen Tatsch, both of Llano, opened some more doors, and some of them were very important ones. The Llano Public Library made its files of unpublished material available to me. Wallace Hazlewood of Llano, who camped with Frank Dobie on the slopes of Packsaddle in the 1930's, confirmed some long-held suspicions. Ellen Hartgrove Sims and her daughter, Mrs. Fred Campbell, of Paint Rock, gave me access to the priceless Indian rock paintings on their ranch, which have been shamefully mutilated by vandalism in recent years. Clyde and Eddith Harlow of Calf Creek took a stranger on a tour of their place and showed me what may well be the real site of the Calf Creek Fight. Dan Feather in Menard gave me access to information about the Comanche Princess. This list could go on for pages — John Crabtree in Dallas, who walked in one day with an 1840 map of the Red Hills and dumped it in my lap, saying "Hey, Craze, I know you like old junk"; "The Jedge" who provided the charter of Los Almagres — I'd never finish. Thanks to all.

Preface

"History is a falsehood sworn to by two liars, both of whom are dead." So said Ambrose Bierce, the Devil's lexicographer, in the years before he annoyed Pancho Villa and wound up as a pile of anonymous bones moldering alongside a dirt road in northern Mexico. Let me substitute a new definition. History is a skeleton. Legend is flesh. Legend—and legend includes oral history never attested to by the two dead liars and never confirmed by a live one with a Ph.D. after his name—is what makes history worth reading. The Alamo is history. Travis' sword-drawn line in the dust has been fairly well confirmed as legend. What would the story of the Alamo be without Jim Bowie's cry of "Carry me over, boys," issued from the cot on which he would die?

Most of this book is legend, but I include only those legends that have some sort of confirmation—somebody dug a hole and found something and brought it back and some other folks saw it. You will read no stories here that end: "An' I looked down the hole an' I seen a big pile a silver bars with thishere skeleton layin' over 'em, an' then I looked back over my shoulder an' the Injuns was awful close, so I lit a shuck outa there an' I ain't been able to find thatair hole since."

This is the story of the Lost San Saba/Los Almagres/Las Iguanas/Lost Jim Bowie Mine. I have, understandably, raided Texas' primary source of lost mine legend, J. Frank Dobie. I've also done a lot of digging on my own, and in doing so I've confirmed a lot of Dobie's stories (stories he never bothered to confirm himself) and I've dug up a few he missed, and digging up what Dobie missed means digging deep.

In the hot summer of 1948 Ralph Doyal first told me the tale of the Calf Creek Fight as his granddaddy, Matt Doyal, who was with Jim Bowie in the ring of rocks, told it to him. In the hot summer of 1980, thirty-two years later, the first draft of this book saw light. Ralph has been dead almost thirteen years, and my greatest regret is that he never got to see where his story led me. His wife, Ruby Capps Doyal, hewn as solidly out of Mason County granite as Ralph was, still lives in Austin, and it is my hope that this book will bring her as much pleasure in the reading as it did me in the researching and writing.

C. F. Eckhardt
Seguin, Texas

How the Lost San Saba Mine
Came to Hunt Me

Somewhere, a long ride past the sunset, there is a range so wide and beautiful that the chosen few who enjoy its pleasures never wish to leave. The mountains that border its plains are higher and bluer than all others, and the water in the streams is colder than the north wind and sweeter than honey. The air is clear and clean, and the smells are those of cedar, pine, mesquite coals, and the blessed aroma of the spring-like rains that fall just often enough to keep the grass green and succulent and never long or hard enough to make a saddle uncomfortable.

The air has the property of healing ills: the ravages of old age and arthritis—even the seared lungs that are the legacy of mustard gas. The land is always green, the rain gentle and timely, the breeze soft and fresh and cool, and the grass, no matter how heavily grazed by buffalo and longhorned cattle, is always belly-high on a tall horse.

He rides that range now, still leather-tough and wind-lined, but his lungs don't burn and his joints don't ache. He rides a tall horse that never tires, and he sits a good—not fancy, but good—saddle with a wide horn and Texas-square skirts. He pulls the horse to a stop, pushes back his hat, and while the horse crops the lush grass contentedly, he looks at me.

"I told you it was there, boy," he says. "All you had to do was keep looking."

Somewhere out there he drinks scalding black coffee from a tin cup, pouring it out of a granite pot that has a green mesquite twig laid across the top to keep it from boiling out—a dry one won't work. He taught me that, and a lot more. Maybe someday, if I am very lucky, I'll ride with him, and he and I will journey to those far mountains, where under a granite ledge we'll find a lode of silver that is all the legends say it should be.

His name is Ralph A. Doyal. He gave me, some thirty years ago, the greatest gift a man can give a boy. He gave me a dream.

I had the great misfortune to be a kid who was sick a lot. Every spring for as long as I can remember, I spent the last four or five weeks of school and the first couple of weeks of summer in bed with a malady the doctors called by whatever name was popular at the moment—strep throat, asthmatic bronchitis, you name it. I still get this mysterious ailment about once or twice a year and the doctors have finally quit trying to put a name on it. They just ask me if I've got it again, I say I have, and they shoot me full of antibiotics until it goes away.

When my bouts with Virus X began, television, as far as central Texas was concerned, was an exotic contraption found only in the Buck Rogers comic strips. I did a lot of reading during those six or seven weeks of bed rest, but *Walt Disney's Comics and Stories* and *Roy Rogers Comics* could keep me entertained only so long. And, because my mother was a schoolteacher who refused to allow pulp magazines in our home, I was unwittingly denied the last great boom in American short fiction. Mother made up for this, however, by bringing me books from the school library and the public library, and—wonder of wonders—out-of-adoption texts from the school bookroom. We had some wonderful texts in those days. I met Frank Buck in *Bring 'Em Back Alive*, Jim Gillette in *Six Years with the Texas Rangers*, and Jim Bowie, Davy Crockett, William B. Travis, Sam Houston, Jim Bonham, and many others in a slim volume titled *Texas Heroes*.

Nineteen forty-eight must have been a good year, for during that year's convalescence from whatever-it-was I received a book that hadn't made its first stop on someone else's shelves. The author of the small, dark-blue volume was J. Frank Dobie, and the book was *On the Open Range*, a selection of essays excerpted from several of Dobie's classics, among them *The Mustangs, The Longhorns, A Vaquero of the Brush Country,* and, most important, *Coronado's Children.* This led me, almost immediately to the unabridged version of *Coronado's Children,* and from there to a *metate* marked EXCAVAD and finally to the Lost San Saba Mine.

In an article I wrote for *Treasure Search Magazine* several years ago, I characterized myself as one of Coronado's illegitimate nephews. It takes more, I said, than rumor to get me excited. While that may be true today, it wasn't true in 1948. No sooner had I read the tale of the *metate* and been introduced to the tales of the Lost San Saba Mine than I became as true a blood son of Don Francisco Vásquez de Coronado as ever tramped a pasture, a glint of gold in his eyes. I spent that summer bubbling over with lost mines and buried treasure. I mentioned it—mentioned it? I ran it into the ground as only an obsessed eight-year-old can—in the presence of our neighbor, Ralph Doyal.

Ralph was one of those characters that come along maybe once a century, mostly because there isn't enough hard rock exposed in a hundred years to carve more than one. When I first met him, he worked for the government at Bergstrom Air Force Base near Austin, and in later years he was a guard at the Texas State Capitol. Those were the occupations of a man who had already lived the lives of ten men and was just taking it easy as old age approached.

A cowboy in Mason County during the early years of the twentieth century, when the scars of what some folks call the Mason County War were still fresh, his family had been deeply enmeshed in the history of Texas' Red Hills for two long generations. His grandfather, Matthew A. Doyal, "Old Matt Doyal," rode with Jim Bowie as early as the late 1820's, fought for Texas in the revolution of 1836 and with Indians and anybody else who wanted a fight all over the Hill Country. His dad, Young Matt, fought for the Confederacy and against carpetbaggers, Indians, rustlers, and bandits, and carved his mark in Mason County granite. Ralph came from the same mold.

In 1917 he volunteered for the army—for the cavalry, naturally, since he was born and bred to a saddle in the Texas hills, as familiar with horses and horsemanship as with his own name. The army, however, had other ideas. By US Army regulations there was too much of Ralph Doyal to go into the cavalry—fully outfitted with uniform, weapons, and issue tack, he exceeded the maximum weight allowance for a cavalry horse on campaign. Never mind that Private Doyal had been a professional horsebreaker and spent most of his life astride horses; by regs he was too heavy for a horse soldier. He was issued a typewriter instead.

Private Doyal spent six long weeks forcing his rope-burned and rein-callused fingers to meet the keys of a Remington Standard, while outside his window city boys, whose sole experience with horses had been watching a spavined nag pull the ragman's cart through the tenements, broke bone after bone trying to wring out some of the wildest and woolliest broncs horsetraders ever unloaded on the army. After six weeks of broken arms, legs, backs, ribs, collarbones, what-have-you, and a full hospital, somebody finally got smart and pulled the bronc twister out of the office and put him in the saddle where he belonged. Injuries dropped dramatically as Private Doyal wrung the kinks out of the bangtails before they were turned over to the recruits.

Then the wheels of army bureaucracy ground round and it was decreed that Doyal was going to Georgia to learn to fight the army way. He did, and in a training accident his lungs were fried with mustard gas. He was shipped home, and for the rest of his life every breath he drew brought him a sharp reminder of a training field in the pines of north Georgia.

One summer evening in 1948, while we sat in the backyard because it was too stiflingly hot to go indoors until midnight or after, Ralph Doyal started the Lost San Saba Mine to hunting me. "I reckon I know a little bit 'bout ol' Jim Bowie an' that silver," he said, "seein' as how my granddaddy helped him bury it."

His tale was the beginning of a thirty-two-year search, both physically and in every book and publication I could lay hand to, for every legend, tale, fact, and piece of evidence, physical, legendary, or documentary, that I could find about the Lost San Saba Mine. Other stories sidetracked me from time to time, but I kept coming back to the silver mine in the Red Hills. Now I've found it.

Before we go any farther, let's get something straight. One of the best ways to start a fight is to say you did something and then have somebody say you didn't, because what you say you did doesn't jibe with what he thinks you did. I try to avoid fights these days because I'm getting older and bruises hurt longer than they used to. The Lost San Saba Mine, for the purposes of this book, is defined as La Cueva de San José del Alcazar, discovered in the side of Cerro del Almagre, one-fourth of a league north and west of the junction of Río de las Chanas and Arroyo San Miguel, in February/March of 1756, by Bernardo de Miranda y Flores, *teniente-general de la provincia de Tejas*, and so reported by that individual to Don Jacinto de Barrios y Juaregui, governor of the province of Texas, in the document popularly known as the "Miranda Report." There is room for argument in this definition, I know.

Today all these spots have different names. Río de las Chanas is the Llano River. Arroyo San Miguel is known as Honey Creek. Cerro del Almagre is Riley Mountain. La Cueva de San José del Alcazar is known as the Boyd Shaft. It isn't the only mine shaft along Honey Creek and it is by no means the only hole in Llano County or the Hill Country from which silver has been mined. There are others that perhaps have a better right to be called the "Lost San Saba Mine," but this hole is the first evidence of the attempt by white men to exploit the mineral promise of the Red Hills—as yet still largely untouched—and the first evidence of white penetration into the Red Hills. It is the hole that started all the stories, the single most legendary spot in the Texas Hill Country. It is the Lost San Saba Mine.

Twenty years ago I realized that I was not the first to hunt this lost mine, and would not be the first to find it were I successful. The Lost San Saba Mine has been lost, found, lost, and found again dozens, if not hundreds of times, by many people, some of whom realized what it was and some of whom did not. Fifteen years or so ago I realized that this particular lost mine, at least, was worked out, rich only in history.

At this point you are perfectly justified in asking, "Why, for Heaven's sake, did you keep hunting for something you knew wasn't really lost, and that you figured to be worthless in any case?" The question is fair and deserves a fair answer.

Anywhere in the world that those strange, sunburned, windlined people with faraway looks in their eyes gather and begin to swap their tales, there are six stories you are bound to hear. One, the story of the lost mines of Ophir (King Solomon's Mines) is African. Two are European: the Crown Jewels of England that King John dropped in the Wash, and the mysterious drowned city of Ys on France's northern coast. Three are in the southwestern United States: the Lost Dutchman Mine on or around Superstition Mountain in Arizona, the Lost Adams Diggings in Sno-Ta-Hay canyon on the Arizona–New Mexico border, and the Lost San Saba Mine of Texas' Red Hills.

There are those who will dispute this list, perhaps with good reason. They may add Breyfogle's gold ledge in the dry Panamints; Tayopa in northern Sonora; the Lost Padre Mine in the Franklin Mountains in El Paso; the mine so well known that it is simply called La Mina Perdida ("the lost mine"); the treasures interred in the riverbed with the corpse of Attila, Scourge of God; Genghis Khan's burial treasure; the treasures in the tombs of the pharaohs or the emperors of old Cathay; Zurzura, the lost Crusader city of the Sahara; the lost cities of the D'jebel Harb ("the empty place") in the Saudi Arabian desert; the caravan cities of the Gobi; the seven cities of Cibola; or the wealth of El Dorado somewhere in the jungles of Brazil. They may add European or Asian or Australian lodes or treasures I've never heard about. But they will include, at the very least, Ophir, the

Lost Dutchman, and the Lost San Saba.

When you stand in the entrance to the Lost San Saba Mine you are surrounded by the fabric of legend, adventure, and romance. You can't take a guided tour of King Solomon's Mines. The Lost Dutchman, if it ever was a mine at all (and there is reason to believe that it may not have been), is still lost. You can't watch Son et Lumière at Camelot, and despite the legends, you can't actually hear the bells of Ys. You can, however, stand at the entrance to the Lost San Saba Mine. The experience is almost unique—kin, I should imagine, to entering the tomb of Tutankhamen for the first time.

No, I don't have gold fever, nor do I have its second cousin, silver fever. What I have is a terminal case of adventure fever, and it has led me, at last, to the mouth of a hole in the Red Hills, to the full story of the Lost San Saba Mine and, if I'm lucky, on to something even better.

Now let's back up a little and think about something. The Lost San Saba Mine is empty—worked out. But where in all the world was there a major mineral strike in just one hole? Go to Tombstone and count the shafts. Go to Austin, Nevada, where Pony Express rider Bob Haslam's horse stumbled over a chunk of silver. Go to Colorado, to California, to Alaska, to the Black Hills. Go to South Africa or to the goldfields of Western Australia. Do you find just one mine—or do you find dozens? The Lost San Saba is empty, but was it the only mine there was?

A legend can be compared to a teen-aged girl of the 1950's all decked out in formal regalia for the Senior Prom—a lot of decoration, exaggeration, and downright falsehood separates what the eye beholds from the cold facts. What follows is legend, not fact. I will not, in this recounting of the legend of the Lost San Saba Mine, give any attention to that which is clearly impossible.

As an example of same, an old man in Mason—who honestly believed every word he told me, and was convinced that the great truth he had from his daddy ranked only slightly behind the truths of Matthew, Mark, Luke, and John—solemnly assured me that Jim Bowie and his men repelled the Indians at the battle of Calf Creek because they commanded Colt six-shooters and Winchester repeaters while the Indians didn't.

Now, the historically accepted date for the Calf Creek Fight is November 1831, the exact day being open to question. The Patent Repeating Firearms Company of Paterson, New Jersey (whose president, chief designer, and head sales agent was one Sam Colt), produced the first "Paterson Colt" five-shot revolvers in 1836. The first commercial six-shooters, "Colt's 1st Model Dragoon Revolver," hit the market twelve years later in 1848, after the Patent Repeating Firearms Company had gone bust (later to be revived in time for the Mexican War by a government contract for revolvers). The Henry Repeating Rifle, the immediate predecessor of the Winchester, saw light early in 1862. If the Calf Creek Fight took place in 1831, it predated five-shooters by five years, six-guns by seventeen years, and Winchesters by thirty-one years.

There are many such impossible legends in Texas, some of which place well-known historical figures where they could not have been when they were supposed to have been there, because they were demonstrably somewhere else at the time. This does not, however, deter the teller of such tales from believing them implicitly, despite the facts.

As the purpose of this book is the making of sense out of legend, it is necessary to relate the tale in question. Back in the 1750's Don Bernardo Miranda, the military commander of

Texas, traveled with a strong force of Spaniards out from San Antonio into the red granite hills to the north. Like Coronado before him, he was looking for gold and silver. Unlike Coronado, he found what he was looking for.

Not far from the junction of the Llano and Colorado rivers, General Miranda came upon a high red hill, which he named Cerro del Almagre. In his exploration of the hill he discovered a natural cave of considerable depth and named it La Cueva de San José del Alcazar. Inside the chamber, in plain sight, he found a tremendous vein of nearly pure silver almost six feet wide, from which it was possible to remove chunks of ore as big as the huge, ferocious-looking but cowardly iguana lizards of Mexico. For that reason, the mine is sometimes called Las Iguanas. Don Bernardo wrote a long report, called the "Miranda Report," and as a result Spanish officials decided to mine this tremendous silver strike.

The Spaniards established a mission and a fort near the silver mine. Unsuspecting Indians who gathered at the mission to be instructed in the worship of the Christian God suddenly found themselves enslaved and forced into the mine tunnels to dig silver day and night. Their women and children were compelled to labor in the smelter, melting the ore and refining the silver, which was molded into fifty-pound bars. Occasionally some of this silver was shipped to Mexico, but most of it was stockpiled in a huge chamber or treasure room deep within the mine. This stockpile was hidden even from the Spanish royal inspectors, who were led to believe that the mine was producing much less silver than it actually was.

This course of action continued for many years, while the Spanish priests and the military commander at the fort grew wealthy. A great church was built with Indian labor and adorned with jewel-encrusted statues of the saints and ornaments, while the fixtures of the church, priests' quarters, and Spanish commandant's apartments were made of pure gold and silver from the mine.

Finally, the Indians revolted, killing every priest, soldier, and Spaniard at the mine, church, and fort. They took all the silver, fine *santos*, and gold and silver fixtures, and hid them in a cross-shaped room deep inside the mine. They pulled down the church stone by stone and scattered the fragments. They filled in the mine except for one secret entrance and forever afterwards they guarded that passage to the blood-tainted treasure, killing all white men who came near it.

In the 1820's the legendary Jim Bowie, great adventurer and knife-fighter, came to Texas in search of the Spanish silver. Since the Lipan Indians were the guardians of the mine and treasure, he set out to learn their secret. To that end, he joined the Lipans, living among them, fighting in their battles, marrying one of their women and fathering a half-Lipan son, and finally becoming an Indian in all but color by submitting to a long and painful adoption rite. And still he was not taken to see the hidden mine and treasure. Not until he presented his adopted Indian father, Chief Xolic, with a rifle heavily encrusted with silver, thus demonstrating his disdain for the white man's idea of wealth, was Bowie shown what he had been living among the Indians for years to see.

At last Bowie was taken to the secret entrance to the mine, not far from the ruins of the old Spanish fort; deep inside a narrow and twisting tunnel he viewed a fabulous treasure-trove of stacks upon stacks of silver bars, bejeweled golden images, golden church trappings and personal gear, and across the cavern, gleaming in the torchlight, a vein of almost pure silver.

Naturally, Bowie deserted the Lipans at the first opportunity and hurried back to San Antonio, where he gathered together a small army of frontiersmen, including his brother Rezin P Bowie, Cephas K. Ham, Tom McCaslin, Matthew A. Doyal, and others. He and his men, armed to the teeth, set out into Indian country to seize and work the fabulous mine. They arrived unmolested by Indians, and found that they literally could cut slabs of silver out of the vein with their belt knives and tomahawks. Upon their return to San Antonio, Bowie and his friends discovered that their silver harvest was so pure it could be spent like coinage.

Surprisingly, so long as Xolic lived, Bowie and his men could visit the mine in safety. Though he did not approve of what Bowie had done, Xolic regarded the white man as his son and would not allow the Lipans to accost him or his companions. Xolic was an old man, however, and he died soon after Bowie reopened the mine. He was succeeded as chief by a young warrior named Tres Manos—"Three Hands." When Tres Manos was still a boy, his father had been captured by white men and tortured to death. Among other torments, white men cut off the Indian's right hand. The boy found the hand, cured it in smoke like a green hide, and when it was flinty-hard bored a hole in the wrist and wore the mummified hand around his neck on a thong to remind him of what the white men had done to his father. He hated all whites, and he especially hated James Bowie, the adopted Lipan, because Bowie had once humiliated him in front of the tribe by beating him in a wrestling match.

On Bowie's last trip to the mine, after he and his men had once again filled their saddlebags with the ore, the group was attacked near the secret entrance to the tunnel by a group of Lipans under the leadership of Tres Manos. In the ensuing fight more than a hundred Indians, including Tres Manos himself, were killed, with only one white man, Tom McCaslin, killed, and two wounded. The victors returned to San Antonio, and shortly afterward James Bowie, the only one of the group to know the whole secret of how to find the mine's hidden entrance, was killed in the Alamo. Thus, the secret of the Lipans died with Bowie, and the mine and the treasure were lost forever.

Since that time many people have stumbled onto the secret entrance—almost always in times of great stress. Likewise, they have been forced to leave their discovery under circumstances that required they take little regard of their surroundings, and while these unfortunate souls knew what they found and even had a general notion of where they found it, no one has ever been able to make his way back to the Lost San Saba/Lost Jim Bowie Mine.

This is the legend of the Lost San Saba Mine as related over campfires and in print throughout the years. This is the story that has inspired several generations of Texans to stick their arms, legs, and noses into God-knows-how-many rattlesnake-infested crevices over a stretch of land at least a hundred miles square, all in an attempt to find Jim Bowie's lost silver.

Behind every legend there is a framework of fact. It has to be there, or upon what was the legend built? Sometimes the facts are so old and obscure that only the vaguest outline of truth can be determined; sometimes the veneer of legend is so thin that the facts can be determined almost at once.

In the case of the Lost San Saba Mine, some of the facts are plain, some are obscure, and some, for years considered to be the absolute truth, under scrutiny dissolve into rumor and legend. Let us, then, examine the "facts," and see what sense can be made of the lore of the Lost San Saba Mine.

CHAPTER II
The Journal of Bernardo de Miranda y Flores
February 27–March 10, 1756

The source document
for the Lost San Saba Mine, the starting
point for every search and story ever
to get anywhere at all, is a document

called the "Miranda Report." Surprisingly, few people have read it, save for the few fragments excerpted by H. C. Bolton in *Texas in the Middle Eighteenth Century* and Dobie in *Coronado's Children*. As a result, most people know virtually nothing more than that it is a document, written in archaic Spanish, and attributable to one Don Bernardo de Miranda, who was a Spanish lieutenant-general in Texas in the 1750's.

Bernardo de Miranda y Flores was a thirty-seven-year-old soldier of fortune when he led an expedition into the Red Hills in search of silver. He was born about 1719, but it would be more interesting, for several reasons, to know his birthplace. All really lucrative political appointments were reserved for Spanish-born appointees. Mexican-born Spaniards, even those of impeccable pedigree and great talent, were not considered capable of handling more than very minor political appointments. We do know that he was a professional soldier, and that he joined the army by enlisting, probably in San Antonio, which seems to have been his base of operations.

Apparently Miranda, as he is known, was not a man of wealth; he was definitely not of the *hidalgo* class—"gentlemen" did not enlist as private soldiers in the Spanish provincial army. He was, however, an extremely bright and efficient young man, for by the age of thirty-five he had risen to the rank of *sargento-mayor* of the militias of Coahuila, equivalent to a division command sergeant major in today's US Army. He also inspired the confidence of high government officials to the extent that he became a sort of agent-inquisitory for military affairs. As early as 1752 he was involved in the investigation of the scandal at Ranchería Grande, near present Rockdale, and in late 1754–early 1755, he was involved in another investigation at the old Spanish capital of Texas, Los Adaes (near present Robeline, Louisiana).

At one point in his career Miranda visited the silver mines in the province of Nuevo León, and so presumably knew the

16

difference between silver ore and plain dirt. In August 1755, five Spanish adventurers from the village of San Fernando de Bexar, the fort town of Presidio San Antonio, reported silver prospects in the Red Hills north of San Fernando, near a creek called Arroyo San Miguel, not far from the junction of Río de las Chanas and Río Colorado. Casting around for someone trustworthy to check out the reported silver strike, the governor of Texas, Don Jacinto de Barrios y Juaregui, hit on Bernardo de Miranda, an efficient, effective, and reasonably honest soldier. In a major break with tradition—virtually all Spanish officers were commissioned through family connections or bought their commissions outright for cash—the governor promoted the *sargento-mayor* to the rank of *teniente-general*. The operative title here is *teniente* ("lieutenant"). Miranda's functional rank was about that of first lieutenant in the US Army of the Indian War days, a rank that carried a lot more weight than a whitebar first john these days. The word "general" merely indicated that he was empowered to act in the general province, rather than having his authority restricted to one area.

Miranda was not riding into the unknown when he set out for the silver strike in Cerro del Almagre. As previously noted, in August 1755 five citizens of San Fernando had opened a prospect hole in the side of a hill near a *potrero* or "box canyon" at the head of a creek called Arroyo de San Miguel ("St. Michael's Creek") or Arroyo de los Almagres ("Red Hematite Creek"). By the blind chance of good fortune, that *potrero*, still known by some old-timers as El Potrero, is the only true box canyon in the Red Hills. The five citizens reported some good prospects of silver before they quit the area, possibly because of Indians.

On November 26, 1755, Barrios assigned Miranda to explore the area and report on whatever he found, with special attention to be paid to any and all prospects of minerals. He was given 250 pesos to hire four or five *gentes inteligentes y prácticas* to guide him to the strike, and authority to demand that the captains of the *presidios* at Los Adaes, La Bahía (Goliad), San Xavier (recently relocated from Ranchería Grande at Rockdale to the site of present San Marcos), and San Antonio de Bexar each furnish him with seven mounted soldiers; the captains of the latter three *presidios* were ordered to accompany him on the expedition as well.

Miranda, as was typical of a Spanish bureaucrat, either military or civilian, chose not to lose any money on this deal. Rather than pay 50 pesos per man, he bargained with Andres Ramón, José Miguel Seguín, and Cristobal Chirino, citizens of San Fernando, and hired them for 12½ pesos each. Later he managed to persuade San Fernando city councilman Luís Antonio Menchaca and a Saltillo resident named José de Avila to accompany him, apparently for the fresh air and exercise. He did expend some 20 pesos to secure the services of a Spanish-speaking Indian named José Antonio Caraveo, an interpreter who had grown up among the Apaches and thus spoke Athabascan and possibly other Indian languages as well. Presumably he pocketed the rest of the money, as was his privilege.

Military instructions, no matter whose army or what century, become open to interpretation once they leave the commander's office. Such was the case with Miranda's demand for manpower: Los Adaes sent four soldiers. San Xavier provided five. San Antonio, closer to the governor's eye, sent the full complement of seven. La Bahía sent none. Of the commandants of the three *presidios* in Texas proper (San Xavier, San Antonio, and La Bahía), all found reasons not to leave their commands. What should have been a thirty-eight-man expedition—a very large Spanish expedition for the time—was drastically reduced before it even got started.

We may assume, of course, that no *presidio* sent its candidates for the eighteenth-century equivalent of soldier of the month. It is endemic to the mind of a senior noncommissioned officer of any army or century that the command "send seven men" cannot possibly mean "send seven good men." Such an open-ended call for bodies provides the top sergeant with an excellent excuse to dump his duds in someone else's lap. And, while the soldiers were mounted, we can also assume that they did not ride out on the best horses available. No transportation sergeant sends his best transport out with the garrison's ne'er-do-wells. Miranda's report is shot through with complaints about tired, footsore horses.

On the morning of February 17, 1756, the Miranda party, at least twenty-three strong—Miranda, the five civilians, the interpreter, and sixteen soldiers, probably with pack animals and spare mounts and presumably with a few unrecorded slaves to do the camp work—set out from San Fernando de Bexar for the prospect of Los Almagres. It was both the worst and best possible time to mount an expedition. February and March are usually the wettest, coldest, dirtiest months in a central Texas winter. Gullywasher thunderstorms, flash floods, tornadoes, freezes, rain, hail, sleet, and snow are all possible during this period. That made the timing bad; Indians seldom stirred during February and March, primarily because of the weather, and that made it good.

Miranda measured the distance of his march in Spanish leagues. A league is approximately equivalent to three US statute miles or a little less than five kilometers. Miranda's leagues, however, were "measured" more by wild guess than anything else. We know he had no surveying equipment, but don't know exactly how he made his measurements. By measuring the distance between identifiable points along his route we know that his leagues vary widely, from a little under two miles on level ground to noticeably less than a mile in rough going. Miranda reports, for instance, that between two in the afternoon and sunset on his first day of travel he covered a distance of four leagues (twelve miles). Since the sun would have set around six o'clock, he would have to have been traveling about three miles per hour—excellent time for a caravan not yet trail-wise. In fact, he made only about two miles per hour for a total of eight miles. The following day he reported six leagues of travel (eighteen miles), but we know his camping place was Payayas Pass, a point on Cibolo Creek just east of present Bulverde, Texas—not over ten miles from his previous night's stop.

Miranda's journal is made up of a series of legal documents called *autos*, the best translation of which is "writ." Each entry begins "On the [X] day of said month and year . . ." and ends "So that it might be on record, I put this through judicial proceedings, which I signed along with my attendant witnesses according to law, to which I certify," followed by three signatures, Miranda's and usually Seguín's and Ramón's. In the interest of space such formalities are omitted here, and each day's entry is simply preceded by the date. Following each entry is an explanation, in today's terms, of who-what-when-where.

February 17

From two in the afternoon until sunset, we traveled north, and we arrived at the waterhole they call El Paredón, about four leagues from Villa de San Fernando.

(About eight miles of travel. El Paredón waterhole was a well-known point along one of the many creeks in the Bexar area. Rather than being a real waterhole, like a *tinaja*, it was a deep pool in a flowing creek.)

February 18

I commanded the march to proceed north because the knowledgeable ones assured me that the *almagre* was discovered approximately to the northwest. Having traveled most of the day on the cited course with difficulty, over very rocky dry creeks and a road of rough cobbles, we arrived at the pass known as Payaya, where I commanded that a halt be made for the night. We have seen nothing worth mentioning. This place of the Payaya must be six leagues from El Paredón and ten from the Villa de San Fernando.

(The "knowledgeable ones" were apparently Seguín, Ramón, and Chirino, of whom at least Seguín had been in the party of five who had made the original find. Miranda is off in his direction. Los Almagres lies almost due north, slightly east if anything, of the center of San Antonio. Payaya Pass is the place where Cibolo Creek comes down off the Balcones Escarpment, right on the present Bexar County line, in the vicinity of the US Hwy 281 bridge in Bulverde. It was named for the Payaya Indians, a minor Coahuiltecan band.)

February 19

I commanded that we proceed on the same course as on the day before. Having left the pass of the Payaya and going past the Balcones, we arrived at the river they call Alarcón. This was an effort because of the many hills and rocks, the many *arroyos* formed by the hills, and some thickets that contain valuable cedar and oak timber. This river must be about six leagues from the place of the Payaya. I stopped along its banks because heavy rain would not allow me to proceed. All along the main road that leads to San Marcos, San Xavier, and Los Adaes, this Río de Alarcón is known as the Río de Guadalupe, because near this road it unites with the spring of water having this name. Downstream from there it is known as the Río de Guadalupe.

(San Marcos is the San Marcos River site of Presidio San Xavier, within the city limits of present San Marcos. San Xavier is the old Ranchería Grande complex near Rockdale. The road referred to is the "Old Nacogdoches Road" that roughly parallels present I-35 from San Antonio to Austin. Guadalupe Spring is in the vicinity of present Canyon Dam, and Río de Alarcón is now known as the upper Guadalupe.)

February 20

In spite of the difficulties produced by continual rain showers, I started the march and commanded that we proceed north. After many hardships because of the many hills, *arroyos*, and brush, we arrived at a creek generally known as Arroyo Blanco, which joins the Río de San Marcos almost at its source. There is a distance from this creek to the Río de Alarcón of about eight leagues. In all of this region there are no commodities nor anything except good cedar and oak timber, and on the Río de Alarcón already mentioned there are cypress groves, very valuable insofar as it can be determined.

(Arroyo Blanco is the Little Blanco River, not "White Creek," which is the literal translation of the name. There is a White Creek on the route, but it had another name. The "lost cypresses" of the Hill Country are scattered along watercourses in a half-dozen or more counties, as far west as Kimble and as far east as Blanco. They are as unusual as the "lost pines" at Bastrop or the "lost maples" near Hondo. The nearest stands of bald cypress are east of Houston, over two hundred miles to the east.)

February 21

I commanded that we proceed north in spite of the many rains. At a distance of four or five leagues we encountered a creek with much water, good level ground on both banks, and much rock and wood, all useful. The knowledgeable ones assured me that at a very little distance there was an abundant spring of water, permanent and easy to draw from, and good level ground capable of supporting a moderate settlement.

In order not to be detained, I commanded that its inspection be suspended until our return. And if it offers the commodities claimed, I will report with all clarity upon the subject of other things the said creek offers.

I gave it the name of San Antonio de Ahumada and continued to proceed on the same course until reaching some round white hills they call Los Pilones de Seguín. It must be about eight leagues from these hills to the Arroyo Blanco.

(Arroyo de San Antonio de Ahumada [Ahumada Creek] is the upper Blanco River, before it is joined by the Little Blanco. Los Pilones de Seguín [Seguín's Sugarloaves] are Monument Hill and the other white hills around it. For centuries, cone-shaped blocks of sugar sold in Spain and almost all Latin American countries have been known as *piloncillos*. Thus, the word *pilón*, applied to a cone-shaped hill, translates as "sugarloaf.")

February 22

Notwithstanding the very heavy and continual rains, I commanded that we leave this place and continue on the same northerly course. Crossing many swollen creeks and thickets of cedar and oak timber, at a distance of eight leagues we arrived at the Arroyo de los Pedernales, where we remained all that day and the following, the twenty-third, because the heavy rains did not allow us an opportunity to leave.

(Arroyo de los Pedernales is the Pedernales River of today. When inquiring about it in central Texas, you would do well to remember that it is called the "Perd'n'alice," and that no one would recognize the name of the stream if you pronounced it correctly.)

February 24

I commanded that we leave the Arroyo de los Pedernales, following a northwesterly course. Because all the terrain was full of obstacles, many of the horses were tired and footsore from the numerous rocks, and we halted for the night at the pass of the Conde Marrubio, six leagues from the Pedernales. In all this distance I found little worthy of attention.

(The best candidate for Paso del Conde Marrubio is a gap in the hills between the Pedernales and Sandy Creek, roughly corresponding to the heads of Hickory Creek, tributary to the Pedernales, and White Creek, tributary to Sandy Creek. A line projected due north from the Sandy community and another due west from Round Mountain will intersect in the immediate vicinity of this pass.)

February 25

I commanded that the proper course of the twenty-fourth day be followed and about ten in the morning we arrived at a creek they told me was San Miguelito. Without delay we followed the proper course, and about twelve the stream known as San Miguel was reached. Without making an examination, I commanded that we follow a northerly course onward in order to observe the first *almagre*, at which we arrived late because of the broken country and the poor condition of our horses, leaving its examination for the twenty-sixth day. This *almagre* must be about twelve leagues from the pass of the Conde and a little more than fifty from the Presidio San Antonio.

(White Creek, which flows north into Sandy Creek, seems to be Arroyo San Miguelito [St. Mickey's Creek]. Arroyo San Miguel [St. Michael's Creek] is the first of two "Arroyos San Miguel." It is this one that is known today as Sandy Creek. Some old maps from the Republic period call it Arroyo de San José.)

February 26

Having made camp on a creek they told me was also called San Miguel, about a quarter of a league before reaching the *almagre*, I commanded that the examination of the *almagre* and the rest of the terrain get under way. This having been done, I put a digger and some other laborers to work so that the cave could be cleaned out and examined to see if any ore veins could be found. All day was spent in this activity, and as the cleaning progressed a tremendous stratum of ore was observed. Some of its veins continue from north to south and some from east to west. So that all may be done in an appropriate form, I am omitting in these proceedings any expression of other circumstances, saving them for a separate report.

(This second Arroyo San Miguel is the real thing at last—Honey Creek, an east-flowing tributary of the Río de las Chanas or Llano River, which enters the Llano just above its junction with the Colorado. Miranda's use of the word *cueva* ["cave"] has caused more confusion than any other single point in the reports. *Cueva* can mean either of two things: a cave, or an extensive mining stope. The natural assumption, then, is that La Cueva de San José del Alcazar was a natural cave, perhaps somewhat collapsed, and with brush camouflage. That assumption has gotten the better of lots of folks. People have searched every inch of Riley and Packsaddle mountains and all up and down the bed of Honey Creek for a cave—I know, because I was one of them—when what Miranda was talking about was not a *cueva* at all, but a *pozo* ["hole"], at least at first. The Miranda shaft itself is a vertical hole that looks like nothing so much as an attempt to dig an old-fashioned well. La Cueva de San José del Alcazar, when Bernardo de Miranda reached it on the rainy, uncomfortable evening of February 26, 1756, was a hole about six feet in diameter and probably not too much deeper than it was wide.)

25

February 27

I commanded that the work be continued on the cave of *almagre*, to which I gave the name and commanded that it be called San José del Alcazar. I also commanded that on the following day six soldiers be furnished to explore for a long distance off to the west, as it was not feasible to continue the march to examine the other places, because most of the soldiers were now nearly on foot with the horses tired and footsore, and of those who accompanied me there was no one who was able to serve as a guide to discover the other Almagre Grande.

(This other Almagre Grande may have been simply another hill a little further on, or it may have been as far afield as the Permian Red Beds in the present Midland-Odessa area. If it was the latter, it was due to produce mineral wealth, although not silver, in time, as the Permian Basin is one of the biggest oil fields in Texas.)

February 28

I went out toward the west accompanied by six soldiers to examine all the land possible, concerning which there will be a report. And having traveled until nearly two in the afternoon, we saw the high hill they call Santiago. As it was not feasible to examine it because some of the horses of those who accompanied me were now tired, it was necessary to omit this objective and return to the camp.

(The "high hill they call Santiago" is the subject of considerable speculation. It has been suggested that it might have been Enchanted Rock near Fredericksburg, but that is more southwest than west of the location of the hole. In the far northwest corner of Llano County there is a high, rough mountain, the highest point in the county. Its name, taken from its shape, is Smoothingiron Mountain. Had Miranda continued to explore this vicinity he might well have added another chapter to the legend of the mineral wealth of the red hills. One of the creeks near Smoothingiron Mountain is reputed to contain an elusive but very rich deposit of placer gold.

The sharp-eyed reader will note that 1756 was a leap year, and that there is no entry for February 29. Miranda does not explain the omission, though in his later report he states that he traveled twenty leagues between February 28 and March 1. I prefer to think that he made a clerical mistake on the trail and didn't want to go to the trouble and expense of recopying the whole report. Twenty Miranda leagues could be as much as forty miles, and it would be possible to see Smoothingiron Mountain in the distance if you traveled twenty miles or so generally northwest of the mineshaft.)

March 1

I, with only four soldiers, explored all of the Arroyo de San Miguel as far as its junction with the river they call Las Chanas, which I examined as far as its junction with the Colorado, on whose banks I slept. On the following day without crossing the Río Colorado I commanded that the examination be continued northwest between these two rivers. In these activities I spent all of this day. The next day I returned to the camp of San Miguel without finding anything that offers conveniences for settlement, or anything else worthy of attention except many mineral veins wherever a hill was encountered.

(If Miranda didn't cross the Colorado, he had to cross the Llano to avoid retracing his steps. Across the Llano he would have explored the area around present-day Kingsland and may possibly have gotten as far west as modern Llano. It is peculiar that he never mentions the most prominent landmark in the area, Packsaddle Mountain. Packsaddle has its own lost mine, generally called the Lost Blanco Mine. There is a "magic circle" of landmarks on Packsaddle's western slope that is associated with the Lost Blanco Mine, which supposedly dates from the Spanish period. The "magic circle" actually dates from 1860, and is related to a lead mine with a showing of silver.)

March 4

Having seen the examination made and it not being feasible for me to do anything further in a matter of such great importance for the reasons already given and having lost provisions because of the great amount of rain, I commanded that we return to the Presidio San Antonio and that the examination commanded in the writ of the twenty-first of February be made. All the particulars of these activities are to be reported to the governor and the captain-general of this province so that His Lordship can determine what seems convenient to him.

(There are no entries for March 2 and 3. This entry refers to the exploration of the area around the Arroyo de San Antonio de Ahumada [the upper Blanco] and its spring. Miranda's constant references to the bad weather and footsore horses indicate that the expedition was under considerable hardship the entire time.)

March 10

In virtue of these proceedings being concluded, I command that the originals be sent to the governor and captain-general of this province with a separate report concerning all the particulars of this journal and also the examination made of the *almagre* and several creeks as well as the spring of San Antonio de Ahumada.

(There are no entries for March 5 through 9. This last entry was made at San Fernando de Bexar after the expedition reached home.)

This, Miranda's journal, is most often referred to as the "Miranda Report." In fact, it is not. Miranda's report is the following chapter; the chapter after that, also sometimes called the "Miranda Report," is in fact a petition to the viceroy. Obviously this journal leaves a lot of questions unanswered, and only a few of them are answered in the next two documents. Also mentioned in the two subsequent documents are yet more "Miranda Reports," though these have not yet come to light.

All the locations cited in this chapter are based on the explorations of author Herbert C. Bolton, who followed Miranda's tracks in 1907 when the hills north of San Antonio weren't full of $300,000 houses and people were a little less touchy about folks crossing their fences. Bolton made his explorations on horseback, incidentally, but he made them in the late spring when the weather was better.

CHAPTER III
Miranda's Report to Governor Barrios
March 29, 1756

Following the submission of his journal, Miranda also wrote a report to the governor of the province of Texas, Don Jacinto de Barrios y Juaregui.

This highly detailed report furnishes a great deal more information about the character of the country than did the journal, and reveals that it was, in fact, so different that a modern central Texan might have a hard time recognizing his native ground. There were, for instance, practically no mesquite trees. Oddly, at no time in either the journal or the report does Miranda mention the presence of wild game, not even so much as a rabbit shot for the camp kettle. While it is understood that wild animals today are much more plentiful than they were in the days of the Indians, in the seventeenth, eighteenth, and nineteenth centuries, game animals were considered a resource —an exploitable source of food for settlements. As Miranda was very careful to mention all other resources (wood, water, building stone, etc.), it is very peculiar that he did not mention this one. It is, of course, entirely possible that he saw very little or no game. The weather he describes would keep most game animals deep in the thickets, hidden from the driving rain and biting wind.

The report to Governor Barrios is all of a piece, and should be read as such. It does, however, contain a number of references that need to be explained. For that reason, rather than break the narrative with an explanation, I have decided to use a series of footnotes.

SIR:

Until the seventeenth day of February it was not possible for me to put into execution Your Lordship's order of the twenty-sixth of November, as much because of the occurrences in this city council[1] and neighborhood (of which I have given an account to Your Lordship) as because the four soldiers from the royal *presidio*[2] arrived with their horses unfit to make the jour-

---

[1] The San Antonio city council hasn't changed much in two centuries.

[2] Los Adaes.

ney. Besides this, I found the Presidio de San Xavier in the deplorable state that Your Lordship will perceive by the writ of the twentieth of last December. Aside from the severity of the winter, these are the reasons that I was prevented from exe-cuting with the greatest promptness that which Your Lordship dictated in the cited order.

In the first four days I did not find any more than what appears in the proceedings. On the twenty-first day the creek [Ahumada] that I cite in the proceedings was found. On my return I had it inspected as far as the spring of water about which the knowledgeable ones had been telling me and assuring me of its permanence. Having seen and examined it, I found almost a *buey de agua*,[3] capable of supporting a rich farm, whose level areas begin above and below the spring, which is large enough to support a moderate settlement of twenty-five to thirty residents. It has such conveniences as easily withdrawable water, much rock, and cottonwood, oak, and cedar timber, all in considerable amount. They tell me this creek was restricted by the Arroyo de los Pedernales because there is a very large difference in the two. The Arroyo de los Pedernales, which is the one that I cite in the writ of the twenty-second, joins and flows into the Colorado, and this creek [Ahumada], at a short distance from where I passed by it, joins the Arroyo Blanco and the two flow into the Río de San Marcos almost at its source. If it were not for the large volume of water in this creek and the spring of San Antonio de Ahumada, the San Marcos would become dry, because even after many rain showers the Arroyo Blanco did not have a volume of water comparable to this one.[4]

---

[3]A volume of water amounting to several thousand gallons per minute in flow.

[4]Apparently Miranda was unaware that the San Marcos is spring fed along most of its length.

The stream called San Miguel that I cite in the writ of the twenty-fifth is considered useless for a farming settlement, for along as much of it as I examined I failed to find withdrawable water. Even if there was any, there are no level areas that could be irrigated, because of the many *arroyos*, thickets, and hills along its course. Beyond this stream some *quemazones*[5] and mineral veins indicated by much white and variegated gravel begin to appear. The stream could well be used for the working of the mines because of the proximity of the *almagre*, for the four scant leagues[6] distance provides very gentle terrain so that with little trouble the ore could be transported in carts.[7]

The mines that are throughout the Cerro del Almagre and all its slope are so abundant that I guarantee to give a mine to each one of all the inhabitants of the province of Texas without anyone being discriminated against in the surveys, even if they were to flourish and stake off as much as they are permitted by the royal ordinance. I assert, furthermore, that at many of the mines the owners will be able to install *haciendas*[8] in such a way that the entrances to the mines will be right in the *haciendas* so that it will not be necessary to expend one *real*[9] for freightage. I further assure Your Lordship that with about three hands-

---

[5] A *quemazone* is a tracing of black manganese oxide commonly found in connection with a deposit of silver ore. There is another, very similar form of black manganese oxide tracing called "desert varnish" that is not necessarily associated with silver. Black manganese oxide tracings appear in most Hill Country streams and can be recognized by black or dark gray streaks in limestone gravel. Now, how do you tell the difference? As one old-timer put it, "If you find silver, it was *quemazone*. If you don't, it wasn't.

[6] Remember Miranda's leagues. This could be only about three miles.

[7] This is a conflict. Earlier he characterizes the same stream as being unsuitable for irrigation because of a lack of places to draw water.

[8] Not fine houses, but *haciendas de fundición* or "smelters."

[9] One-eighth of a peso, also called "piece of eight" or "bit."

breadths of soil cleaned away they could go in and extract ore similar to that which I am sending to Your Lordship and in such abundance that two furnaces would not be enough to reduce the ore that a single digger could extract.

The other creek called San Miguel,[10] cited in the writ of the twenty-sixth of February, is about a quarter of a league from the *almagre*. It must have a volume of water of about a *buey*, and they assure me that it maintains it during the severest drought. For a distance of more than two leagues to the east, its banks offer some places for withdrawing water, at which they could put in smelter mill channels. This creek begins about a league and a half west of the *almagre*, and at its source is a *potrero* more than three leagues in circumference.

This *potrero* has good grasslands, and the facility for setting posts across some openings or outlets formed by the high hills and placing rails from post to post so that the horses and mules belonging to the owners of the mines can be turned out without fear that they will stray. And it will not be necessary to bother giving them water, for they will have it in this stream, which flows through the *potrero*, and in another creek that flows between west and south, and also in pools capable of being watering places for stock.

Leaving this *potrero* toward the west, there are mineral veins again, although they are much scarcer than at San José del Alcazar. I saw these for most of the ten leagues that I traveled until sighting a high hill they call Santiago, not being able to proceed onward for the reasons cited in the writ of the twenty-eighth of February.

This *potrero* has a flat area of land, good and level and large enough for sowing five or six *fanegas*[11] of maize, and with such

---

[10]Honey Creek.

[11]A *fanega* is equal to about 2½ bushels.

facility for withdrawing water that it can be done without it being necessary to dam the stream. The creek makes a bench or ledge of rock, and the field borders upon the creek; so it is seen how the water can be withdrawn without any trouble.

But I should tell Your Lordship that one must not pay any attention to withdrawable water or to land, because in mining camps one first attends to these rather than to the farmers. And if this water is expended in farming, there is none for mill channels for reducing ore, or for making *planillas*,[12] all of which come first; for Your Lordship is not ignorant of the fact that the royal fifths,[13] rather than the other special interest, are and should be attended to first.

Of the conveniences, not the least are the large and nearby thickets of mesquite[14] and oak, very useful for charcoal. For house building and other necessities needed by *haciendas* for extracting silver, there is much cedar, pecan, cottonwood, and oak timber; and also, wherever they want to open them, rock quarries for houses and for lime.

From this place of the *almagres* to the Río de las Chanas there are about three leagues, and five to the junction with the Colorado. This area offers no commodities of any kind except plentiful and useful timber. From the place of the cave of *almagre* to where they say the Presidio of San Xavier is being put[15] they assure me is a distance of thirty leagues toward the west.

---

[12]The eighteenth-century equivalent of a riffle box.

[13]Income tax—the king got 20 percent of everything.

[14]Mesquite is mentioned nowhere else in any report, so it couldn't have been anywhere near as common as it is today.

[15]This is the San Saba River site of the Presidio San Luis de las Amarillas, just west of Menard. Thirty leagues is ninety miles, but the actual distance is closer to seventy-five miles.

Although I would have liked to have fulfilled my obligation to see and explore all the land of the Apaches, I had no means for the reasons stated, nor did I find any Indian of the Apache nation who would guide me so that I could make other discoveries. In order to succeed in encountering some, I made use of the scheme of setting fire to the field at several places, but this scheme did not produce the desired result until, on the way back, on the Río de Alarcón, a well-known Apache Indian overtook me. He gave me reason to believe that at the source of the Río Colorado, six days' journey from these two *almagres* that I had seen, there were two good deposits of *almagre* that were those they took from for their own use, and that four more days' journey from these two *almagres* was another with two rich ore veins; but in order to go to this one, many Spaniards would be needed. They, together with the Apaches, could go; because if only a few go and the Comanches are living at this *almagre* they could kill them all.[16]

Telling him that I wanted to paint churches and houses with *almagre*,[17] I offered him a blanket, some tobacco, a horse, a bridle, a big knife, and other trifles if he would take me to the *almagres*, because the one I had seen was no good. I used this pretext so that he would not guess the real reason. He gave me his word to conduct me whenever I wanted, and if we came

---

[16]Two points: First, Coronado may have been the first to hear *más allá* from an Indian, but he was by no means the last. Second, what Miranda's Indian is saying is that the Comanches would kill everybody in sight: Apaches, Spaniards, and all.

[17]*Almagre*—red hematite—has been used as a pigment for centuries. The color is a dull red, almost a terra-cotta hue. It also lasts. To this day, the Indian pictographs at Paint Rock show three colors: red (hematite), yellow (ocher), and black (charcoal). There may have been other colors centuries ago, but they have faded, even in those pictographs protected from weathering. The oldest pictographs, estimated at between 3,000 and 4,000 years of age, are painted with hematite, and where protected by overhangs they are brighter and more distinct than the black-paint graffiti painted a mere half-century ago.

every "moon" he would travel with the Spaniards. For this I used the interpreter whom I took along.

Don Luis Menchaca, José de Avila, and the three civilians whom Your Lordship paid to conduct me to the *almagre* presented me with mining claims for ten mines, certification for which I gave them with the conditions for settling when there might be an opportunity for settlement or guard, and the obligation to work them according to royal ordinances.

I am very sorry not to have been able to discover the other Almagre Grande, but Your Lordship must know it is no fault of mine, for with few and badly equipped soldiers and without guides it is not possible to go out successfully on such important discoveries in regions unknown to the Spaniards.

Your Lordship has no news from here. Thanks be to God all minds are peaceful and without lawsuits, disturbances, or quarrels, although at my arrival various writings were presented to me. These are in my charge and will remain so, without any action being taken. This has seemed to me to be a convenient measure to take in order to secure the quiet that is being experienced.

I will rejoice if there is propriety in everything, and if in everything my wishes conform to the pleasure of Your Lordship. Whatever occurs, I still pray that God may guard Your Lordship's life in perfect health for many years.

> Bernardo de Miranda y Flores
> Teniente-general de la provincia de Tejas

With this report Miranda submitted an ore sample weighing about three pounds. It was sent to Mexico City, to the attention of the viceroy. The viceroy gave it to a mine owner named Manuel de Aldaco, and at this point controversy—the controversy that has plagued exploitation of the silver prospects of the Llano country for two centuries—enters the story for the first time.

CHAPTER IV

Miranda's Petition to the Viceroy of Nuevas Filipinas
February 15, 1757

The worst thing to happen to the Los Almagres ore was its falling into the hands of Manuel de Aldaco (sometimes called "Albaco").

In Mexico City, Aldaco had part of Miranda's sample assayed by smelting and explained, in a long, technical report, that he could obtain less than ¹⁄₁₀ ounce of silver from one pound of ore by smelting, and none at all by amalgamation. Assuming Aldaco was being honest, the *almagre* ore was very low grade. Aldaco was a mine owner at Monte, deep in Mexico, and most likely the viceroy himself had invested heavily in Aldaco's mining operations. Such apparent abuse of office was not uncommon in Spanish Texas. It was, in fact, covertly encouraged. Offices were commonly purchased by the officeholder's family, and most often the officeholder's salary—his "hardship"—did not cover his expenses, much less repay the purchase price of the office, even over a lifetime. Spanish politicians were not, as a rule, wealthy, altruistic idealists interested in "good government." The family laid out gold for one member to gain office on the expectation that various goodies would accrue to the family as a result, and they were seldom disappointed. So long as an officeholder didn't tamper with the king's fifth, nobody worried a great deal about what else he did.

Aldaco had a good reason to wish failure on Miranda. If Miranda opened a successful silver mine, and a particularly rich one at that, the viceroy might see fit to deal himself in at the start of the new venture and pull his patronage out from under Aldaco. Failing that, he might decide to demand a bigger slice of Aldaco's pie in exchange for his continued patronage. That is, *if* Miranda's ore proved good. Should it prove poor, that would be another story.

There are a half-dozen versions of Aldaco's assay, and we are free to choose the one we prefer to believe. In an early story, J. Frank Dobie put the assay at 11 troy ounces to the pound of silver ore, very nearly *plata pura*, since there are only 12 troy ounces to the pound. Later, in *Coronado's Children*, Dobie corrected this to 10 ounces per hundredweight, which, while by no means pure silver, was not ore to be dismissed lightly. In *Texas in the Middle Eighteenth Century,* Bolton says that the ore proved "very rich" and that the prospects were "very bright," then goes on without committing himself further.

Aldaco reported that the smelting process yielded $\frac{1}{10}$ of an *onza* (1 *onza* equals approximately 1 troy ounce) of silver from about a pound of ore. Then he hedged, claiming that both the testing vessel and the testing reagent he used were contaminated with silver from a previous test. As a result, he "corrected" his assay to 5 *onzas* per quintal (101 lbs), and then proceeded to test another portion of the sample by amalgamation. Aldaco knew full well that if the ore contained arsenic, the amalgamation process would produce an assay of zero. The amalgamation test indicated a total lack of silver—as it would if the ore were silver arsenate, one of the more common forms of silver ore.

Aldaco presented both assays to the viceroy, and then capped the situation in such a way that Miranda would never be able to get a second opinion. Knowing Miranda to be without personal fortune or patronage, Aldaco suggested to the viceroy that Miranda be required to produce, at his own expense, thirty *cargas* ("mule loads") of ore, to amount to about two quintals weight per *carga.* Ten of these were to come from the surface, ten from a depth of five *varas* (about fourteen feet), and ten from a depth of ten *varas* (about twenty-seven feet). He then suggested that Miranda be required, again at his own expense, to transport six tons of ore overland to the mining complex at Mazapíl, in northern Zacatecas, a mere 260 leagues (780 miles) away, and to pay out of his own pocket the cost of reducing and smelting the ores at the *haciendas de fundición* of Bonanza and Cedros—and guess who owned an interest in both of those legendary smelters? In order to do all this, Miranda would have to mount a second expedition into Indian country, and hire diggers to mine some three tons of ore and then load it on mules for the trip to the smelters—mules that had to be bought and fed by Miranda, naturally. Even if Miranda managed to accumulate enough financial backing to pull it off, there was no assurance that Aldaco wouldn't have another shell game waiting in Mazapíl. Highgrading is as old as mining, and there are hundreds of ways to do it, assuming the ore ever got to Mazapíl. The road to Zacatecas is a long and lonely one even today, and *los muertos no hablan*, especially after their bones have been picked clean by buzzards and scattered by coyotes.

Miranda was apparently a sucker for shell games. He made a trip to Mexico City and requested that he be permitted to see the assay report. On February 1, 1757, he got the bad news.

If Miranda had good silver prospects and knew it (and while he may not have been a miner some of his men were), the trip to Mazapíl would be worth the risk. If he could persuade the viceroy, or somebody, to back the removal of the ore and finance its transport to Mazapíl, then personally shepherd it every step of the way from Los Almagres to Mazapíl, babysit it through the smelting process in order to guard against any sleight-of-hand on Aldaco's part, and finally present the viceroy with bar silver in quantity (about 600 ounces of it if Aldaco's first assay was anywhere near right), Bernardo de Miranda y Flores would emerge a shining star, having beaten Manuel de Aldaco at his own game.

If, on the other hand, Miranda was running a shell game of his own, he would have known that the fun was over right there. If he managed to con the viceroy or some other prominent *rico* into financing the transport of three tons of worthless rock 780 miles into Mexico and lived to tell about it, the name of Bernardo de Miranda wouldn't be worth a plugged *real*. Miranda had to know this, so it is unreasonable to suppose that he would continue to importune the viceroy about Los Almagres if he knew or even suspected that the ore was worthless. The fact that he continued to trouble the viceroy about the prospect is a good indication that the Los Almagres strike was worthwhile.

Another point in Miranda's favor is his disinterest in being a mine owner. He wanted, instead, command of the *presidio* that would be established to protect the mines. The position of *comandante de presidio* was perhaps the most lucrative on the Spanish frontier, with almost unlimited opportunities for graft, but the possibility of obtaining such a command hinged on proving the Los Almagres prospect as a workable silver mine. Miranda knew that if the ore did not pan out there would be no *presidio*. Here is his petition.

Most Excellent Sir:

I, Bernardo de Miranda, resident of this court and *teniente-general* of the province of Texas, Nuevas Filipinas, in the proceedings concerning the discovery of certain minerals in the place called Los Almagres, which I executed by virtue of the commission of Don Jacinto de Barrios y Juaregui, appear before the superiority of Your Excellency according to the best procedure of the law and by the most proper application and say:

I requested and was delivered these proceedings for the purpose that I expressed in my foregoing petition. Because of your great comprehension, Your Excellency is already aware of how much is evident in these and the report of Manuel de Aldaco, which is found from the reverse side of page 19 to page 26, with regard to the *arroyos*, rivers, distances, directions, terrain, water, timber, abundance of mining commodities, and saving of expenses in the reduction of ores. Because of this, I will refrain from repeating the statements in order not to bore Your Excellency.

But I cannot omit that most of the veins run from east to west and some from north to south, and that the principal vein is more than 2 *varas* thick, is visible on the surface for more than 300 *varas*, and extends toward the center of the earth on a slant to the west in great extent, like many others that are distributed for five or six leagues along a straight line. Because there are so many, I dared, in the manner that appears on the reverse side of page 15, to give a mine to each one of the inhabitants of this province. Concerning this, I ought to point out that said inhabitants or civilians being about a hundred, I offer to give, in the respective distance of six leagues along a straight line, this same number of mines with the conveniences presented on the cited page.

According to the statement of the Apache Indians, many more and better mines can be discovered at the two *almagres* that are at the source of the Río Colorado, and many also in the place where the Comanche Indians are found; for the two pockets of ore that are mentioned on the reverse side of page 16 are not ore but silver according to the assertion of the Apache Indians, who explained themselves by telling me that they are white like shoe buckles. [The Turk told Coronado *más allá*, and the Apaches told Miranda the same thing in different words.]

But it is to be kept in mind that for this discovery, although Indian guides are taken along, measures are necessary for making available those men that are needed as well as corresponding orders to the presidial captains so that they can contribute sufficient guards, equipment, and provisions of mouth and war. [Obviously Miranda realized he had been badly burned by the *presidio* commandants on his first expedition, and he had no intention of being burned again.]

It [the need for sufficient funding] is also to be kept in mind, considering the measure that Don Manuel de Aldaco advises concerning the sending of ore to the *haciendas* of Bonanza and Cedros (the thirty loads of ore that Don Manuel advises on page 24), especially when the freightage of each load cannot be lowered to less than twenty pesos considering the distance of 260 leagues that lies between Los Almagres and the *hacienda* of Bonanza, which is the nearest place where the assay of the thirty loads is advised. And even if all of them worked their mining claims, the means would be furnished from the same money that the mines yield to them; and from that method they would begin improving and making themselves capable of building *haciendas de fundición* for the reduction of the ore.

Without doubt, when they dig deeper this ore will increase, not only in richness but in ease of reduction; for not having taken sufficient people for the work or the necessary tools, it was not possible for me to be able to dig deep, and so almost from the surface I crudely removed some ore, which is what was assayed. And even if this had no greater richness than 2 *onzas* per quintal, clearly it would be rich enough that the owners of the mines would become wealthy because of the great saving on freightage, the ease of extraction, and the abundance of charcoal and wood for its reduction. [Miranda obviously decided that a very minor slap at Aldaco was necessary.]

For the provision of the *presidio* that I have proposed, it is also to be borne in mind that in the province of Texas His Majesty has an annual expenditure of 100,000 pesos and said provision can be undertaken without incurring new expenses. And this working of the mines would not only pay this expenditure, but from the royal fifths His Majesty would greatly benefit. The existence of the *presidio* need only be while the mines are being settled with a number of residents capable of defending themselves in case of barbarous Indians. Without such provision it does not seem possible to me that these mines can be worked, for the reasons stated.

And finally, in spite of what I have explained, Your Excellency deigns to order that the assay of the thirty loads of ore and the examination of the other mineral deposits be done in the manner contained in the cited report of Don Manuel de Aldaco, since it is impossible for those who claimed the ten mines to do it, and so that everything may contribute to an augmentation of the royal fifths of His Majesty, the extension of his dominions, and the alleviation of his vassals, I must finally point out to the rectitude of Your Excellency that for freightage alone the cost will not be less than 600 pesos, not counting the salaries of the laborers and the necessary tools, provisions, and horses.

And as I am not able to spend it from my pocket, having only my personal hardship, if these expenses be paid for the account of the royal treasury without, for now, assigning me any honor corresponding to my effort until all that I have expressed is verified—in which case the reward ought to be corresponding and respective to it—I will proceed to execute all that is prescribed in the referred report [Aldaco's] and with people placed at the discovered ore deposit, I will make the other discoveries if I am able to find them, sending their ores to the stated *haciendas* in the proper conformity and separately.

And in case Your Excellency does not regard this proposition to be to your superior liking, I am ready to pay all of it through my industry and perseverance with the condition that I be the captain of the soldiers that are found to be placed at the said mines, and that what they earn be paid to them by me in the same way that other captains do. Thus equipped I will be able to assist those who work the mines so that all will be given in the service of His Majesty, augmenting his royal purse and benefiting the public until there are sufficient residents to defend themselves from the assaults of the Indians.

I pray that the grandeur of Your Excellency will be pleased to make the provision that, in terms of and having its justification in the present laws and dispositions that favor the discoverers of mines, will be most convenient to the royal service and alleviation of the vassals, and let the fiscal [a lawyer who protected the king's financial interests] of His Majesty see it. I humbly pray that Your Excellency be pleased to command as I ask in justice. I make the necessary vows, etc. In addition, I ask that Your Excellency be pleased to command that the transactions that may be necessary in this affair be understood by Don Diego Giraud, resident and merchant in this city, because I have conferred upon him power of attorney for my business and in the rest *ut supra*.

> Lic'do José Ossorio
> [Ossorio was a licensed scribe]
> Bernardo de Miranda y Flores

With this petition, Miranda stuck his head in a noose and, in effect, invited the viceroy and Aldaco to pull it tight if he couldn't deliver. The viceroy, however, declined to pull the rope. He handed the petition over to a functionary who, in true bureaucratic fashion, replied that the first proposal, that the Crown pay for the transport and reduction of the ore, was totally unacceptable. And, the functionary continued, the *presidio* could not be established until after the required ore had been produced, tested, and found rich enough to justify mining, which effectively knocked out Miranda's offer to pay for it out of his own pocket, since he could afford this expense only as a *presidio* captain. Finally, the functionary said, any *presidio* captain would be chosen according to his merits.

Since Miranda had gone back to Texas to try and scare up some investors, this piece of bureaucratic doubletalk was delivered to his representative, Giraud. Giraud, being familiar with Spanish bureaucratese, read this to mean that (a) the viceroy was too deeply invested in Aldaco's mines to want Miranda muddying the water and (b) *presidio* captains were appointed by virtue of their powerful relatives, their political clout, and the bribes they were able to drop in the proper pockets. Working on the principle of pork-barrel politics that says if you can't get a ham at least get an ear, Giraud managed to extract a viceregal promise that if a *presidio* were ever established near the mines, Miranda would command it. This may well be the reason Presidio San Luis was never moved to the Llano.

Within the next few years a *presidio*—San Luis on the San Saba, later Real (Royal) Presidio de San Saba—was established, as was the Mission San Saba, both too far away to be considered connected to the Los Almagres silver strike. Miranda, of course, never got to command that *presidio*—or anywhere else, for that matter. He never made captain, and while he remained in Texas for a number of years and figured prominently in a number of explorations he apparently never found any silver, either.

CHAPTER V

The Other Spaniards in the Hills

The prospect at Los
Almagres was worked, with varying
degrees of intensity, by a number of
Spaniards and possibly one Frenchman,

for about fifty years. A smelter was established, and since a smelter requires an *arrastre* ("ore crusher"), we may safely assume that an *arrastre* was established somewhere in the area. Smelter remains have been tentatively identified in several places, some of which undoubtedly are kitchen middens or frontier campfire sites, but the *arrastre* remains unfound. A slagpile, the unquestionable mark of a Spanish smelter, stood near one smelter site for about seventy-five years, until it was resmelted by Harp Perry and his partner and its remains scattered. Remnants of what might have been the slagpile can be found in a couple of places. Nor was Los Almagres the only prospect worked. At least one other, known as Espinazo de Judas, was prominent enough to have a name.

In 1757 the *presidio* that had been moved from Ranchería Grande near Rockdale to San Marcos was moved for the final time, this time to the San Saba River about seventy-five miles north and west of the prospect of Los Almagres. In March of the following year, about two thousand Indians swooped down on the mission near the *presidio* and burned it, killing two of the three priests and most of the Christianized Indians. The Comanches recorded their feat on the rocks at Concho Canyon, just outside of present Paint Rock.

The Spanish suffered an unmitigated disaster at Mission San Saba, and the Comanches, a tremendous success. The cowardice of Captain Diego Ortiz Parilla, *comandante de presidio* at San Luis, who refused to go to the aid of the mission his *presidio* was established to protect, has been a subject of historical controversy for years.

What has been reported as cowardice may well have been plain good sense. If Ortiz Parilla's garrison had been at full strength, he would have had 100 soldiers. The Indians would have outnumbered the Spaniards by twenty to one. In fact, the garrison was undermanned, as was usual for Spanish garrisons. The *comandante de presidio* was paid, in addition to his own stipend, the salaries of his men. If he was authorized 100 soldiers and maintained only 50, he pocketed the rest of the money and no one asked questions. He also received money for feeding, clothing, and equipping his troops, and what he didn't spend he put in his pocket—which explains why the average Spanish trooper on the frontier ate swill, wore rags, and generally carried a rusty matchlock or miquelet long after the more reliable flintlock muskets replaced them elsewhere. Ortiz Parilla was no better and no worse than his contemporaries. *Comandante de presidio* was a lucrative post; that is why Bernardo de Miranda desperately wanted to be one.

When the Mission San Saba was wiped out, the nominal reason for the existence of Presidio San Luis disappeared. *Presidios* existed to protect *Dios y oro* ("God and gold") or roads. Maintaining a *presidio* almost two hundred miles from the nearest supply base was a touchy and expensive proposition. In 1761, a meeting between Padre Diego Ximenez, president of the College of Querétaro and nominal head of the Texas missions, and several Apache chiefs was held at Presidio San Luis under the protection of Don Felipe de Rabago y Teran, Ortiz Parilla's successor. Though the Spanish agreed to re-establish Mission San Saba, it was never done. Apache missions were organized on the upper reaches of the Nueces, far to the southwest, and in the Big Bend country, but Mission San Saba remained a site overgrown with weeds and exposed to the elements. Today nothing remains but an open field, the remains of the mission scarcely identifiable. There is even some disagreement as to where the mission actually stood. Ruins just west of Menard that are often referred to as those of the Mission San Saba are actually fragments of the *presidio*.

Although Mission San Saba was never re-established and no other mission was erected in the vicinity, Presidio San Luis, later re-named Real Presidio de San Saba, was not abandoned until 1769, eleven years after the official reason for its existence had gone up in smoke. Since with the destruction of the mission there was no God, no gold, and no road to protect—the Comanche Road was a war trail, and led only to trouble—there remained only one reason for the continued maintenance of the *presidio*. That reason was silver.

In 1770 the new governor of Texas, Baron de Ripperda, was told by Menchaca, who was with Miranda in 1756, that Los Almagres was a rich mine. It is alleged that he claimed the ore within was gold, and he may have: Menchaca was a merchant and politician, not a miner. Ripperda asked his superiors in Mexico City to establish a *presidio* of 200 soldiers on the Llano so the mine could be worked, but upon investigation of Aldaco's reports and subsequent documents, the new viceroy denied the request.

The refusal apparently did not discourage Ripperda. In 1778 he sent Simón de Arocha, the *teniente-general* of Texas, to examine Los Almagres and the other prospect called Espinazo de Judas. Arocha secured ore samples that were sent to Mexico City. These apparently collided head on with Aldaco's report and went down in flames.

In 1787 a Frenchman named Alexandre DuPont turned up in San Antonio, having wandered in from New Orleans. On March 1, 1788, he set out to explore the Hill Country and visit the prospect at Los Almagres. On March 10 he camped at a place where he "found a lot of ore on the ground," and then continued his journey, arriving at the abandoned *presidio* on the San Saba on April 3. He returned to San Antonio, secured some financial backing, and on February 2, 1789, took off again, this time accompanied by several persons including some Comanches and leading several mules laden with trade goods. Wandering as far north as the Red River, he may have crossed into Oklahoma and gone as far as the Wichita Mountains near present-day Lawton and Fort Sill, circled back, and around the middle of May, struck what may have been Los Almagres. He sacked up some ore, traveled back to San Antonio (by this time the name "San Antonio" applied to the town as well as the river, the fort, and the mission) for additional mules, and eventually entered Mexico with several mule-loads of some sort of ore. We don't know what became of Monsieur DuPont and his ore, but he apparently never went back to the prospect on Honey Creek if he ever actually got there in the first place.

In the summer of 1789, six men left San Antonio to work the deposit at Los Almagres. In September one returned with a tale of a massacre at the mine in which his five companions had been slaughtered by Apaches. This attack, by Indians supposedly friendly to the Spaniards, took place in August 1789, and was the first of only two Indian attacks ever reported at Los Almagres.

In the summer of 1792, Governor Manuel Muñoz of Texas came under investigation for "irregularities." Whatever his offense, it had to be flagrant, since "irregularities" were the specialty of Spanish political appointees. Either that, or Muñoz stepped, knowingly or unknowingly, on sensitive and highly placed toes. Whatever happened, Manuel de Escandón, governor of Nuevo Santander, took over Texas while Muñoz was being investigated. At that point, Muñoz tried to sneak off into the hills with thirty soldiers, supposedly to "examine the silver prospects at Los Almagres and other places." However, Ramón de Castro, *comandante general* of the Eastern Interior Provinces, forbade the expedition, probably because he feared Muñoz intended to go over the hill and never return.

These were the officially acknowledged attempts to mine Los Almagres. How many more there were, no one knows. According to the Harp Perry story, Perry and his partner were able to resmelt the old slagpile near the Los Almagres site and extract enough silver from the slag alone to set themselves up in a clandestine mining business employing at least twenty-five laborers. This argues for a long and fairly continuous use of the mine and smelter. In addition, the existence of a smelter near the Los Almagres stope argues that someone was taking out ore in large enough quantities to justify building the smelter in the first place and to produce a sizable slagpile through its use. Officially, however, Los Almagres did not exist. A single report, filed in 1757 by a man who had reason to want the mine to fail, effectively torpedoed development of Los Almagres as a recognized major mining complex.

CHAPTER VI
The Mission San Saba
and Presidio San Luis de las Amarillas

The story of the mission and *presidio* on the San Saba River is a long and involved one, a story that has never been and probably can never be fully told. This is true of most history, but there is a special reason for the mystery surrounding the Mission San Saba. According to some historians, the full story is locked within an organization of the most secretive people on earth.

They do not refer to the Comanches, who burned the mission, since the Comanches have never been reluctant to boast of their exploits. What the Comanches remember, they tell and tell proudly. Nor do they refer to the College of Querétaro, which operated the mission, because most of its records are available if you have the right connections. They refer to the people they believe originally built the mission long before its official founding in 1757: the Fathers of the Society of Jesus, or Jesuits.

The official records, the ones to which we have access, indicate that Mission San Saba existed from April 1757 until March 1758, in other words, for eleven months, scarcely enough time to construct much of a mission.

According to Ferdinand von Roemer, a German intellectual who traveled extensively in the "German" part of Texas in the mid to late 1840's, the Mission San Saba consisted, in 1848, of a thick stone wall as much as twenty feet high in places, with a watchtower at each of the corners, encompassing an area 300 feet by 360 feet—well over two acres—and containing a church and fifty stone cell-like *residencias* or dwellings. Again according to von Roemer, at the time he observed the mission, a good half of the major buildings in the town of Menardville (today Menard) had already been built of stone cannibalized from the mission and yet monumental remains still could be seen on the site.

On the basis of this, a good many researchers, realizing that even with modern construction techniques and equipment a complex like the one von Roemer described could not have been built in eleven months, have theorized that the mission had a longer life than its official one. Since the date of the massacre is positively known to have been March 16, 1758, and there is no evidence of any mission activity following that date, the life at San Saba had to precede that date. The Jesuits are known to have built clandestine missions and to have conducted surreptitious mining in Mexico and perhaps in California, Arizona, and New Mexico as well. Therefore, some say, the Jesuits built Mission San Saba.

We might have reason to question this. In von Roemer's book *Texas*, first published in Germany in the 1850's and finally translated into English for the Texas Centennial in 1936, he questions whether there was a separate mission on the San Saba. It becomes apparent, on reading his comments, that he is describing not an unknown mission complex, but the still-standing but somewhat more deteriorated ruins of what is today known as Presidio San Saba—Presidio San Luis de las Amarillas or Real Presidio de San Saba.

Catholic historians universally insist that there were two constructions on the San Saba, a mission and a fort, and that they were situated anywhere from two to nine miles apart. Father Edward W. Heusinger, in his *Early Explorations and Mission Establishments in Texas*, gives the impression that the mission may have been built of wood, with a log-palisade wall like the "cavalry forts" of Hollywood (100,000 perfectly straight lodgepole pine logs that just happen to be lying conveniently in the middle of the Mojave Desert so the US Cavalry can build Fort Apache for the Apaches to burn down with fire arrows). In fact, it was probably built of a combination of logs and adobe, in what we would call mud and wattle construction.

The construction of Mission San Saba—who, when, and to some extent, precisely where—remains open to some doubt. The whole story isn't in yet, and won't be until a full-scale archaeological expedition goes to Menard, locates the actual site of the mission, completes an investigatory dig, and analyzes the finds. According to the records we have, the Spaniards built a church with at least one bell tower and an encompassing wall with *residencias*, dug a well, planted crops, and attracted over three hundred Indians, all in eleven months—remarkable, any way you look at it.

The history of the *presidio* is more thoroughly documented, and while less mysterious, is more interesting. The *presidio* that ultimately stood on the banks of the San Saba River was first established as Presidio San Xavier, alongside Brushy Creek, not far from the present town of Rockdale. It was intended as the center of a *presidio*/mission complex called Ranchería Grande, which was supposed to do for the Río San Xavier (today San Gabriel) area what a similar complex was doing for a site along the San Antonio River. Ranchería Grande was to become the new Bexar, the second in a proposed string of *presidio*/mission complexes intended to consolidate Spain's hold on the province of Texas.

The site was well chosen. The land along Brushy Creek east of present IH-35 is generally extremely fertile, well watered, and easily tilled. The actual site chosen was well drained, and the deep black topsoil produces excellent crops today. There is ample limestone and sandstone for building in the area, and there is, and was, plenty of good hardwood timber for building temporary log buildings until stone ones could be erected.

The plan was to erect a *presidio* and three missions. The short names of the missions, the names they are generally known by today, are San Ildefonso, Candelaria, and Dolores. The *presidio*, named San Xavier, was erected alongside Brushy Creek, a dam was built, and an *acequia* or water ditch was dug. Both the dam and the *acequia* are still in existence, and if you know where to look and what to look for, you can still find the remains of both. The stones of the dam are somewhat scattered, but they are visible when the creek is low and the water clear. There are pecan trees three feet in diameter and larger growing in the *acequia*, but the ditch is distinct enough to be noticed, and Ditch Valley Farm, on the site of one of the missions, takes its name from the canal.

The three missions were built and over two hundred Indians seem to have turned up almost overnight. As was customary, the missions catered to different tribes. One served fringe Apaches; one the Tonkawas; and one a group of related Karankawan groups that came in from further east. From all appearances, Ranchería Grande was well on its way to becoming a new Bexar.

In less than five years it was abandoned. The Indians were gone, the buildings were falling to ruin, the fields were abandoned to weeds, and the Spaniards had returned to Bexar. For many years students of Texas history were told that Ranchería Grande collapsed because the Indians were too nomadic, warlike, and downright lazy to take to mission life. In fact, the reason Ranchería Grande collapsed was a man—two men, in fact—and a woman. Ranchería Grande was the scene of Texas' first sex-and-murder scandal.

Don Felipe de Rabago y Teran, *comandante de presidio* at San Xavier, was a typical Spanish aristocrat. As such, he considered Indians something less than human. Indian men, anyway; Indian women he considered as toys for his men. He apparently urged his troops to enjoy themselves with the more attractive Indian women available at the three missions.

This, of course, distressed the *padres*. They were having enough trouble putting their charges into pants and dresses and imbuing them with the doctrines of Christianity, not the least of which were the one-woman-per-man rule and the sanctity of marriage. The Apaches, in particular, were having trouble with the pants. They insisted on cutting the important part out of their mission-issue breeches and wearing them with their loincloths as leggins.

To add to the problem, the soldiers were helping themselves to the Indian women without regard for Christian or native marriage vows, and the commandant was encouraging them to do so. It was too much to be borne. The priests protested to their superiors in Mexico City, including a request that Rabago y Teran be relieved of duty and a that a new commandant be appointed.

Don Felipe, who had charge of the mail pouch, read the protest and counterattacked. There were, he said, very few Indians at the missions, not nearly enough to justify three missions and the priests to staff them. It would be wise, he suggested, to consolidate the missions into one, the one nearest the fort, and to recall most of the priests, since there were, in effect, more priests than Indians. Although not one word of Rabago y Teran's charges was true—there were actually between fifty and a hundred Indians at each mission and the numbers were growing daily—serious consideration was given to his suggestions, and the *padres* heard about it.

Incensed, the clergy leveled its ultimate threat: excommunication. The *padres* threatened to excommunicate everybody, Don Felipe and all the soldiers included, unless the fun and games with the Indian women ceased immediately. Don Felipe replied by reporting to Mexico City that some of the priests had gone mad and by repeating his request for consolidation of the missions. The priests carried out their threat, posting a notice of excommunication on the door of each church and refusing to hear confessions or administer the host, and the stage was set for Act 2.

As far as the Indian women went, the *padres* might as well have protested to the sky or the river. Spaniards had been taking liberties with Indian women for better than two centuries—a practice begun by Columbus and elevated to a high art by Hernán Cortés and his Aztec mistress, Malinche. An entire social class in Mexico, the *mestizos* or "mixed bloods," had been created by the practice. Undoubtedly many if not most of the pure-blooded Spaniards who were Rabago y Teran's superiors had Indian or *mestizo* mistresses. Unless the soldiers, and Don Felipe, had done something more serious, relieving an *hidalgo* officer of his command was unthinkable.

In the meantime another situation, much stickier from Mexico City's point of view, was developing. There was a white woman, a married white woman, at the *presidio*. While Indian women were of no consequence so far as Don Felipe's superiors were concerned, the commandment "Thou shalt not monkey with another Spaniard's wife" with the qualification "and get caught at it" in small print was virtually graven in stone. And this was exactly what Don Felipe de Rabago y Teran had been doing, ever since he set eyes on the lady.

She was, so they say, the wife of Juan José Zevallos, one of the soldiers. Other accounts indicate that Zevallos was a Spanish civilian, but his presence at a frontier military/religious outpost has never been explained.

They also say she was young and beautiful. Even if she wasn't, the fact that she was the only Spanish-speaking woman in ten days' travel across hostile country in any direction would have made her interesting. Besides, she made it easy for the commandant. As the story goes, she made the march from Bexar with the soldiers, and she was already sharing Don Felipe's fire and blankets before they ever got to the San Xavier site. Be that as it may, by the time the houses were erected at San Xavier she had moved in, body and baggage, with Rabago y Teran.

The husband protested, probably first to the *comandante*, who ignored him. He took his protests to the priests, who in turn protested to Don Felipe, who laughed. Señora Zevallos, whose first name has not come down to us, stayed firmly in the arms, affections, and bed of the *comandante*.

The protests probably got a little shrill, because Rabago y Teran decided to demonstrate his mastery of the woman and her husband, as well as his contempt for the priests, with a display of his power. He had Zevallos arrested and chained to the wall or the floor—accounts differ—of the guardhouse hut by his wrists, ankles, and neck. Rabago y Teran moved in several candles and a bed. Then he led in Señora Zevallos, stripped her naked, had her strip him, and in the words of the official historian "proceeded to debauch the woman in a most disgusting manner while her unfortunate husband looked on, unable to interfere." After he had enjoyed himself for an hour or so, he dressed, wrapped the naked woman in a blanket, blew out the candles, and led her back to his quarters. The next morning he had the husband released.

Zevallos took his story straight to the *padres*, in particular to a Padre Ganzabal, who seems to have been one of the bigger thorns in Don Felipe's side. Padre Ganzabal took a deposition from Zevallos and prepared to send it to Mexico City.

Ganzabal had Rabago y Teran by the short hair, and both of them knew it. Mexico City might overlook a lot, but not this. Unfortunately for Zevallos and the *padre*, the only way to send the deposition to Mexico City was in the military courier's pouch, and since Don Felipe controlled the military, he also controlled the mail. Shortly afterward, on Christmas Day, Zevallos and Padre Ganzabal were murdered in the doorway of Mission Candelaria, the soldier with a close-range blast from a musket loaded with buck and ball, the *padre* with an arrow. The deposition vanished.

That was enough for the Indians. They had tolerated a lot from the crazy white men, but when they took to murdering their own kind, especially inside their god's house on his greatest feast day, it was time to leave. Within a week Don Felipe's earlier reports had come true—there were, for all practical purposes, more priests than Indians. In addition, according to the report of one of the priests, there were signs and portents in the sky, the crops were blighted, the creek dried up, and the cows went dry.

Some weeks later an Indian turned up in San Fernando, or more likely at Presidio San Antonio, and confessed—without torture, according to the report—to the murder of the priest. A soldier was tried and convicted for the shooting of Zevallos and both were executed. After an investigation, Rabago y Teran was relieved of his command (one of the investigating team appears to have been the *sargento-mayor* of the militias of Texas, Bernardo de Miranda y Flores) and a new, less priapic *comandante* replaced him. The damage, however, could not be undone. Presidio San Xavier and the Ranchería Grande mission complex were doomed. Within a very few years the Spaniards marched away from Brushy Creek, never to return, and the *presidio* was re-established at a site along the Río San Marcos on the Nacogdoches Road within what is now the city of San Marcos.

In 1960, in my quest for everything I could find out about the San Saba Mine, I visited Ranchería Grande. I found the man who owns Ditch Valley Farm and most of the land on which the Presidio San Xavier and its closest mission stood. He pointed out to me the *acequia* and showed me where, under the rushing, muddy water of Brushy Creek, the remains of the old dam were. Then he told me an interesting tale. When he was a small boy, back before World War I, downstream from the dam near the site of Mission San Ildefonso there was a large, deep, quiet pool—a swimming hole. He, his brothers, cousins, and friends swam there often. At the bottom of the hole, he told me, some fifteen or eighteen feet down, there was a big iron pipe of some kind, a pipe with curiously thick sides. He could remember trying to dive all the way to the bottom of the swimming hole so he could grab the pipe before coming up. Now what, he wondered, would a big iron pipe have been doing at the bottom of a swimming hole in Brushy Creek, miles from an improved road, in 1914?

Pipe? There were certainly cannon at San Xavier. In the 1750's, Spaniards dragged cannon with them everywhere they went. Suppose that when time came to pull out, one of the cannon couldn't be moved thanks to a broken wheel, rotten carriage, or too few horses to pull the old-style carriage without a limber—it takes ten to twelve horses to pull a gun without a limber, while the same gun, with the end of its trail balanced on a limber cart, can be pulled with four. There was no time to make a new wheel, repair or replace the carriage, or round up horses. Far better to roll the thing off into a deep hole in the creek. The Indians weren't well enough versed in engineering to haul a ton and a half of metal out of the muck, but they were well enough versed in warfare to figure out how to make it fire and to turn it on the Spaniards at some later date. I looked at the cold, muddy, rushing water of Brushy Creek, higher than usual in spring rains, shivered in the chill of a raw, early April wind, and decided against going skinny-dipping. The cannon, if it is a cannon, is still there so far as I know.

By 1755 Presidio San Xavier was on the San Marcos River, where it wasn't needed, and everybody in the know realized that it was there until someone made a decision either to put it someplace else or to terminate its existence. While it was there, in the spring of 1756, Bernardo de Miranda y Flores, the newly promoted *teniente-general* of Texas, presented the *comandante de presidio* with a demand that the *comandante* and seven soldiers accompany him on an expedition into the Red Hills in search of silver prospects.

The new commandant at San Marcos had a familiar name— Rabago y Teran. It wasn't Don Felipe, but it was his brother, and as a result of the investigation at San Xavier, in which Bernardo de Miranda had apparently played an important part, there was a blot on the Rabago y Teran family name. Don Felipe had, in a sense, walked away. No actual crimes had been proved against him, and he still had his military rank. Still, he had been relieved of his command, which never looks good on a soldier's record. If Bernardo de Miranda, an upstart who had conned his way into a commission rather than buying it like proper gentle-men did, had anything at all to do with brother Felipe's getting canned—and since his promotion to *teniente-general* came pretty much on the heels of the investigation he probably did—there was no way Don Felipe's brother was going to give him anything but the back of his hand. The commandant of San Xavier-on-the-San Marcos sent four soldiers on spavined horses. He re-fused the governor's order to accompany the expedition.

In April 1757, thirteen months after Miranda mounted his expedition into the Llano country, Presidio San Xavier was moved to the San Saba River and renamed Presidio San Luis de las Amarillas. Diego Ortiz Parilla was named commandant. This had been planned for quite some time, and Miranda mentioned the move in his report to the governor. He was, however, a little unsure of the exact location, because he said, "From the cave of *almagre* to where they say the Presidio de San Xavier is being put they assure me is a distance of thirty leagues toward the west." The distance is, in fact, more like twenty-five leagues, or seventy-five miles rather than ninety.

By the spring of 1758, the eleven-month miracle having been wrought, there existed on the San Saba both an operating mission and a fort manned, nominally, by a hundred soldiers, although there were actually only about fifty troops on hand. The construction of the mission has already been discussed, and to chase that rabbit down any more holes would be useless. We do know that there was a mission compound with a church having at least one bell tower, a compound wall of some sort, *residencias* or housing within the wall, a well, a farm, and stock pens. One source, James Wakefield Burke's *A Forgotten Glory—The Missions of Old Texas*, tells us that there were 237 Indian women and children, mostly of the various Apache bands, at the mission, together with an indeterminate number of Indian men to a total of "several hundred." While one might tend to doubt such specific figures, a guess of three hundred to three hundred fifty Indians, all told, at Mission San Saba would probably be reasonably accurate. Another source, probably somewhat less reliable, gives the number at "around 600," and a third source, which has consistently underestimated and underplayed the accomplishments of the mission enterprises in Texas, insists that there were fewer than one hundred Indians there. Burke is probably as accurate as we'll get. There were also at least eight Spaniards at the mission itself—Padres Alonso Giraldo de Terreros, José Santiesteban, and Miguel Molina, and five soldiers. Four were José García, Lazaro de Ayala, Enrique Gutiérrez, and Ascendo Cadena. The name of the fifth soldier remains a mystery. At the *presidio*, about two miles to the east and, according to some reports, in plain sight of the mission, there were forty-five to fifty Spanish soldiers under the command of Captain Diego Ortiz Parilla.

In early February 1758 it became fairly obvious to the old Indian-fighting hands at both the mission and the fort that something big, and probably bad, was in the wind. The young men, those who did most of the farm and stock work, were deserting the mission in twos and threes. It was apparent that they weren't just out hunting, as they took only their Indian garments and possessions, leaving their "white man clothes," crucifixes, and other evidence of their association with white men behind. The horses they rode out on and such tools as could easily be converted to weapons were the only mission property disappearing with them. By mid-March, mission activities were at a virtual standstill. The only Indians remaining were some 230 women and children, none of whom were capable of heavy work like strengthening the defenses of the mission or of putting up more than a token fight in its defense. The farm work continued on a reduced scale, and livestock, particularly the mission's horses and mules, disappeared daily.

By the early morning of March 16, it had become painfully obvious that something was wrong. Though work call had been sounded, the mission Indians huddled in the *residencias*, reluctant to leave the walls. Persuasion did nothing to move them, and from time to time a keening later frontiersmen would come to know as death songs arose from the old women.

At about noon the plain to the northwest of the mission was suddenly covered with horsemen as better than two thousand Indians advanced on the mission and *presidio*. They did not charge, nor did they give vent to wild war yells. They surged forward in ominous silence, broken only by the occasional clink of metal and underscored by the rolling thunder from the hooves of their war-painted ponies.

Most sources identify the Indians as Comanche, Apache, Tawakoni, Toyavase, Bidai, and Wichita. Since the Comanches felt about the Apaches, and the Apaches felt about the Comanches, as the French felt about the Germans in 1917, it is unlikely that the two tribes joined in any common undertaking. Most likely the warriors were mostly Comanches, heavily armed, both with native weapons and with a scattering of European muskets, pikes, swords, and lances. Every warrior was in full war regalia and fully painted.

The approach of the Indians both alarmed and confused the Spaniards. The *padres* prudently closed the gate, as did the soldiers at the *presidio*, in plain sight two miles to the east. The five soldiers at the mission entertained no illusions about their fate if the Indians decided to storm the mud and stick walls. They primed their muskets, loosened their swords, and prayed.

At the *presidio* Captain Ortiz Parilla had a bear by the tail. His job was to protect the mission. He had perhaps fifty soldiers, each of whom was armed with a single-shot musket that took almost a minute to fire, reload, and fire again, and could be expected to misfire one try in six. If he marched out to meet the Indians, the job he was paid to do, his command would last about five minutes. The soldiers would get off one volley, perhaps two, and then it would be swords and socket bayonets, fifty against two thousand, and in considerably less time than it would take to write the story, fifty Spanish scalps would be dangling from Comanche war shields and lances. One of those scalps would be the mortal remains of Captain Diego Ortiz Parilla. Inside the *presidio* walls the Spaniards at least had a chance. The army sat tight.

Back at the mission, everyone was confused except the Indians, who knew exactly what was going to happen. The chiefs of the war band began to protest loudly. Why, they demanded, had their friends barred the gates? They didn't ride against Spaniards—they liked Spaniards. They were a war party, but they rode against a common enemy to the southeast, the Tonkawas. They had come to ask their friends for horses and mules as spare mounts for their warriors, and if the *padres* happened to have any food and tobacco they'd like to have that, as well.

The mention of the Tonkawas was a deft touch. There was one proved tribe of cannibals in Texas, the Karankawas, but every tribe—except the Tonkawas—insisted the Tonkawas were another. No one ever proved the Tonkawas ate human flesh, but enough suspicion had been raised over the years to give the *padres* gooseflesh at the name. The Comanches had thrown all off guard, when they needed to be very much on guard.

Soldier Ascendo Cadena recognized several Comanches with whom he thought he had made friends. He realized, of course, as did everyone else, that the Indians could take the mission if they wanted to, and there was nothing five muskets, or even the *presidio's* fifty muskets, could do to stop them. But, not being a seasoned Indian-fighter, he argued it was better to open the gates, give them what they wanted, and send them on their way. Padre Alonso agreed. The gate was opened and the Indians swarmed in. Padre José, perhaps more pessimistic or more realistic than Padre Alonso and Cadena, went into the mission chapel, knelt at the altar, and began to pray for the souls of the Spaniards and Christianized Indians at Mission San Saba.

Outside, some of the Indians began to shake hands with the Spaniards and protest friendship. Others, apparently more anxious to get on with the business at hand, began to loot the place. The mission's horses and mules, not many by this time, were rounded up and driven away.

There were not enough. The Comanches wanted more horses—many more. They were a big war party, going to put an end to the eaters-of-men once and for all. How could they fight without horses?

Somebody, probably the garrulous Cadena, pointed to the *presidio*. There were many horses and mules there. If the Comanches were truly friendly, if the looting stopped, perhaps Captain Ortiz Parilla could be persuaded to lend some of his horses.

Perhaps a hundred warriors set out for the *presidio*. As they came within musket range of the walls it became obvious that Captain Ortiz Parilla was not going to lend the Comanches his horses. He didn't even intend to let them get close enough to discuss the matter. A volley crashed and the *presidio's* cannon roared. The range was still too great for accurate shooting, but perhaps a half-dozen Indians fell. The rest turned and rode back to the mission.

Perhaps the gunfire from the *presidio* was what the Comanches had been waiting for, for almost as if it were a signal the massacre began. We have the word of only one man, Padre Miguel Molina, as to what happened next.

Cadena and Padre Alonso Giraldo de Terreros were shot down and hacked to pieces. Padre José Santiesteban, still on his knees praying in the chapel, was beheaded by a sword stroke. His head was thrown in the mission compound, and several Indians began to kick it about like a soccer ball. The remaining four soldiers were shot down and hacked to bits before they could get off a shot.

Padre Miguel Molina, the last white man alive, grabbed eight mission Indians and barricaded his party in one of the *residencias*. The *residencias* were dwellings within the walls, very much like monks' cells but larger. Each had a heavy wooden door that could be barricaded from the inside, and there were no windows. Unfortunately, the roofs were highly flammable brush. Padre Miguel and his charges were ignored for a time, but as the looting and burning progressed the roofs of the *residencias* were set afire.

The mission cattle were turned out of their pens, slaughtered, and left to rot. The women, mostly Apaches, were stripped, raped, murdered, and chopped to pieces. Younger children and babies were seized by the heels and their heads dashed against the walls of the chapel. Older children were stabbed or hacked to death. The images of the saints were pulled from their niches and smashed, and everything portable was taken, either to be destroyed or carried away.

About dusk the fire reached the cell that hid Padre Miguel and his eight terrified charges in the *residencia*. As the heat became unbearable, he offered a final prayer for salvation, unbarred the door, and the last nine Christians alive at Mission San Saba bolted for the *presidio*. Five were shot or run down and killed before the party got halfway. The rest, including Padre Miguel, made it to the *presidio* walls. They alone lived to tell the tale.

Back at the mission everything that would burn had been set fire, and every animal that twitched and every human being that whimpered was given an extra blow with a sword or a tomahawk to make sure. The last bodies were stripped and mutilated, and in the gathering dark, the war party rode away to the northwest.

They stopped, either the night of the seventeenth or the eighteenth, in the canyon of the Concho River, just north of present Paint Rock. There on the rocks of the canyon wall, where their allies, enemies, and ancestors had been recording their triumphs and tragedies for almost three thousand years, they recorded their deed. The pictograph is still there today, perhaps somewhat faded but easily noticed.

The Comanche artist who depicted the events of some two and a quarter centuries ago appears, however, to have made two very significant errors. So far as we know—and we don't know much, as this is the only likeness of the Mission San Saba known to exist—the mission on the San Saba had a single tower. In the rock painting a building with two towers is in flames. In addition, the now weathered painting originally showed three dead priests. While there were three priests at Mission San Saba, only two were killed—the third, Padre Miguel Molina, escaped to the *presidio* under cover of darkness. It is possible that the artist assumed that the third priest also died in the massacre and thereby painted a representation of him standing on his head (the symbol for a dead man), but the origin of the two-towered building is open to question. The pictographs at Paint Rock are not merely records of accomplishment. They are messages to the gods, and as such, inaccuracy and artistic license would not have been encouraged. If the tribe killed twenty white men and took three women captive, the gods wanted to see twenty inverted figures and three skirted figures lying on their sides (the symbol for a captive), not forty and six. If a mission with one tower was burned, the gods would not look favorably on a painting that depicted a mission with two towers aflame. There are two possibilities here. Most likely, the artist did not join in the actual raid and painted from hearsay. Less likely, this is the only surviving record of a completely different, otherwise unrecorded mission massacre. There were missions on the Nueces and in the Big Bend country that were massacred, and no Spaniard survived to tell the story. Could this be the only record of one of those? No white man knows,

71

and if the Comanches remember they aren't telling.

Incidentally, a punitive expedition of about three hundred well-armed soldiers was launched toward the northwest. They found rather more Comanches than they were prepared to tangle with under any circumstances and returned to San Antonio sooner than had been planned.

Shortly after the massacre at Mission San Saba, Comandante de Presidio Diego Ortiz Parilla made an official request of his superiors in Mexico City. His *presidio*, he said, was ill placed and useless unless someone was foolish enough to try to re-activate Mission San Saba. It would be better, he argued, to remove the *presidio* to the Río de las Chanas (the Llano) where it would serve to encourage the working of the reported silver strikes along that river and its tributaries by affording protection against marauding Indians. He was to make that request twice more before he was replaced, in 1760, by the new commandant—our old friend, Don Felipe de Rabago y Teran. Mission San Saba remained abandoned.

In 1769 Presidio San Saba was inspected by a military team from Mexico City. They found that although commandant Rabago y Teran was authorized seventy-five soldiers, he actually maintained only thirty. Of these, several were so deeply in debt to the commandant that they had not been paid in three years. Two of those in debt were so old that they were entitled to retire, but were unable to do so because of their indebtedness. The soldiers were in rags, and their food was terrible. Their weapons were so poorly maintained that over half the muskets either would not fire or could reasonably be expected to blow up in the soldiers' hands if they were fired. The team recommended that Don Felipe be removed from command and that Presidio San Saba be abandoned. In 1769 the Spaniards marched away from Real Presidio de San Saba for the last time, and the San Saba experiment became history.

Today the ruins of Presidio San Saba, for the most part preserved in a state of "arrested decay" with some reconstruction, can be seen adjacent to a golf course, on the western edge of the town of Menard. A few hundred yards to the south the clear waters of the San Saba flow over the same rocks the Spaniards knew two and a quarter centuries ago. Somewhere, and the authorities disagree as to exactly where, there is an open field, and somewhere on that field there is an unmarked cemetery. In that cemetery are buried the remains of Padre José Santiesteban, Padre Alonso Giraldo de Terreros, soldiers Ascendo Cadena, José García, Lazaro de Ayala, Enrique Gutiérrez, and one other, and some 230 Christianized Apache women and children. They are all that remains of Mission San Saba.

CHAPTER VII

Los Almagres
Becomes the Lost San Saba Mine

L os Almagres was never
on a map, since it never officially existed.
Real Presidio de San Saba, seventy-
five miles to the northwest, appeared

on Spanish, Mexican, and later English maps, usually marked as Presidio San Saba, old *presidio*, or old Spanish fort. As time passed, the ruins of Real Presidio de San Saba began to take on a mistaken identification with the "silver mine of the hills." As the location became more firmly misestablished with the passing years, Spaniards, Mexicans, and later Anglo Texicans began to build legends of a lost mine of silver and gold and later—much later, after 1866—about a lost treasure-trove of silver bars in a cave somewhere on the scrub oak-covered limestone plain near where Menard now stands. Although many of those legends today are connected to James Bowie, research will show anyone who is interested that the cave full of silver bars story did not crop up until 1866, and that the connecting of this tale to Jim Bowie didn't take place until romantic fictioneers discovered the "romance of Texas" after the turn of the twentieth century. Today—and for about the last 120 years—the Los Almagres silver strike on Honey Creek near the junction of the Llano and Colorado rivers is known as the "Lost San Saba Mine," although it is nowhere near the San Saba River, Mission or Presidio San Saba, Old San Saba Fort (which is not Presidio San Saba), Camp San Saba, or the present city or county of San Saba.

The beginnings of this confusion can be traced to one Juan Antonio Padilla, who reported in San Antonio in 1819 that there were rich deposits of silver near the Colorado northwest of San Antonio, but that they could not be worked. They were, he insisted, well known to and well guarded by the Comanches, who feared the Spaniards would enslave them and make them work the mine. Since Comanches, so far as is known, had never been successfully enslaved, it would appear that Padilla was blending the Los Almagres story with the legends of La Mina del Padre (the Lost Padre Mine). In the Franklin Mountains north of El Paso del Norte, La Mina del Padre was supposed to have been sealed during the 1680 Indian revolt, and remains lost, though the generally accepted location is known. That gold mine was supposedly filled by the Indians who had been enslaved to work it and was guarded not merely by living Indians, but by the ghosts of the Indians who died working it as well as a Spanish *patrón*: the ghost of a Spanish prisoner who was buried alive in the mineshaft.

While Padilla started the confusion, Stephen Fuller Austin allowed it to mature. Erasmo Seguín, father of San Jacinto hero Juan N. Seguín, was Austin's duenna on the future Father of Texas' first trip to the province. Seguín filled Austin's ears with stories of a rich silver mine on the San Saba River and a "gold dust" mine on the Llano—both of which, it turned out in later years, were quite real. Whether or not Austin, the supreme real estate promoter, bit on Seguín's hook is unknown, but he used the same bait to catch his own fish.

There can be no question that Austin knew about the old mission and fort on the San Saba, since it was clearly marked on Spanish maps of the area. For reasons of his own, mostly because he thought it would sell real estate, Austin marked the *presidio* location on his 1829 map with the words "Silver Mine." In 1831 his brochure on Texas boosted the San Saba River as the traditional location of rich silver mines that flourished until the Comanches overran them and wiped out the workers—a neat, if totally fictional, blend of either Los Almagres or Las Iguanas with the Mission San Saba disaster of 1758. It is strangely coincidental that Austin should have done this, since the Las Iguanas mining complex near the old *presidio* was almost completely unknown to Texans until the digging began on Silver Creek in 1866.

Mary Austin Holley, in her 1833 book *Texas*, picked up the story almost without alteration, and she was followed by Almonte the next year. By the 1840's, when the Adelsverein began to purchase land in the Red Hills, one of the selling points used by the promoters was "rich mines of silver and gold" not far from the area where the German settlers were to move. At least in part, these rumors prompted von Roemer to explore and report on the area.

By the time John Arrowsmith produced his Texas map in

London in the 1840's, the mine had wandered even further west. Arrowsmith's map shows the location of Presidio San Saba on the San Saba River as "Old Fort," and far out on the Concho River near the present site of San Angelo, Tom Green County, he placed the magic words "Silver Mine." Since then the mine has continued its meanderings. Some associate it with another legendary silver mine, also connected with a Spanish mission and located on the upper Nueces. Even J. Frank Dobie, that formidable searcher after lost mine lore, has suggested, in *Coronado's Children*, that it might be reasonable to hunt the Lost San Saba beyond the Pecos (which Arrowsmith managed to transmogrify into Río de los Puercos or Hog River).

Most searchers, though, have concentrated on what is loosely defined as the San Saba area and covers a hundred-mile or so strip along both sides of the San Saba River, from its junction with the Colorado in San Saba County to the site of the old US Cavalry outpost at Ft. McKavett, west of Menard. The name "San Saba" appears along this strip of land eight times—the city and county, the San Saba River itself, San Saba Creek in the county of the same name, Camp San Saba community in McCulloch County south of Brady, Old San Saba Fort between Brady and Menard, and the mission and *presidio* of San Saba in Menard County— more often than any other single place name in Texas. For all that, we still don't know what it means, for there was no saint named Saba. The most likely guess is that the word *saba* is an archaic term deriving either from the verb *saber* ("to know") or from the noun *sabiduría* ("wisdom"), and that the term means "holy wisdom" or something very close to it.

Meanwhile, back in Mexico, the Spaniards had been thrown out in an eleven-year revolution that left most of the people who knew where and what Los Almagres was either dead or on the run. When Mexico temporarily settled down under the rule of Agustín Iturbide, the self-styled Iturbide I, emperor of Mexico, a Mexico City resident named Salvador Carrasco bent the emperor's ear about a rich deposit of silver and gold in the hills northwest of San Antonio that could not be worked because of hostile Indians. Carrasco sent his remarks on the silver and gold "about forty leagues, more or less, from the city of San Antonio de Bexar" through proper channels. His letter, dated May 25, 1822, went up the ladder, receiving endorsements in July, August, and November of the same year. On January 22, 1823, Sebastian Rodríquez Biedma, a regular army captain and director of the military academy at Monclova, forwarded Carrasco's letter with an endorsement that contained some personal comment about the silver. Captain Rodríquez first heard of the mines while stationed at Corpus Christi. He later assayed specimens of ore while he was in San Antonio and found them rich. He requested that the emperor station a detachment of 350 cavalry at Los Almagres.

On March 19, 1823, Emperor Iturbide I abdicated the throne of Mexico one jump ahead of a firing squad. Los Almagres was forgotten in the confusion. There is a rumor that Iturbide did send an adventurer named José de la Baume, together with two soldiers, to find and inspect the mine, but the time factor makes la Baume's expedition unlikely.

All during the Mexican period, the period of the Republic, and into early statehood numerous explorations were launched into the San Saba country in search of silver and gold. Most of them were misaimed and concentrated near Menard, and a few were simply covers for other activity. We shall see later how the Bowie brothers used the lost mine story to cover silver "mining" of a different sort. Since none of these efforts—except Bowie's—met with any success, the Lost San Saba Mine began a retreat into the realm of myth, and those who had been to the Menard area and realized that the limestone formations near the old *presidio* were hardly likely to contain mineral wealth began to regard the whole thing as pure fancy. They were wrong, but at that time no one knew it.

Following the War between the States all sorts of tales began to trickle out of Mexico, as Mexicans, driven beyond the Río Grande by revolution and terror, fled to Texas bringing half-remembered legend with them. A map and a *derrotero* ("waybill") turned up in San Marcos in 1866, brought up from the cathedral at Monclova by an old Mexican woman named Carlota. According to legend, the Monclova cathedral's archives are the repository of a tremendous amount of "Texas silver" information, supposedly jealously guarded by the priests. Since the College of Querétaro controlled the Texas missions under the Spanish, the legend may have some basis in fact.

Carlota's *derrotero* called for an oak tree with a chunk of flint in a three-forked crotch, a series of copper pegs buried at thirty-*vara* (one *vara* equals thirty-three inches) intervals to form a triangle, and a broken *metate* or corn-grinding stone. The location was three leagues west of the Presidio San Saba and one league north of the river, up a tributary today called Silver Creek. The items called for were actually found, the flint rock grown deeply into the tree and the copper pegs heavily tarnished and pitted with age. The *metate*, when assembled, had the word EXCAVAD ("dig") deeply incised into the grinding surface.

The instruction "dig" didn't mean a Sunday afternoon's work. The *derrotero* called for the clearing out of a pit some seventy feet deep, followed by several hundred yards of twisting tunnels that would lead to the treasure room containing 2,000 bars of silver. The searchers picked a likely spot and began to dig, and people are still digging there, more than a hundred years later. The silver indicated by the *derrotero*—both the legendary "cave full of silver bars" (this marks the first appearance of that) and a rich silver mine to boot—is, like the elusive pirate hoard on Oak Island, "still there, just out of reach."

A later tale has every appearance of being a swindle that never quite came off. The pigeon was a doctor in Mills County, north of San Saba, and the scam involved a vast treasure supposedly hidden by the priests of Mission San Saba, which was said to be the banking mission for all the wealth gathered by other missions in Texas. This tale has added fuel to the idea of the Jesuits as builders of Mission San Saba. Since the mission is known to have existed for a mere eleven months, it is unlikely that it ever served such a purpose, even ignoring its isolated location.

Following directions given by a young, aristocratic-looking Mexican, the doctor dug up a couple of large copper disks and a copper box. The disks, known in legend as the "copper plates," were inscribed with pictographs that the doctor interpreted as indicating a vast treasure of gold, silver, and jewels hidden in a cave, but for several reasons the sting did not progress past the digging up of the plates. The amazing thing about the whole scam is the fact that the doctor failed to note that the copper objects he dug up were untarnished. Mission San Saba was abandoned in 1758. The *presidio* was abandoned in 1769. The last Spaniards left Texas in 1821; the last Mexican officials in 1836. The plates were unearthed in the late 1890's. Supposedly they were underground for at least 60 years, and more likely 80 or 120 years. One would have to suppose that copper objects buried for a century or so would develop some sort of patina, at least.

As Arthur and the Knights of the Round Table are the Matter of Britain, the Song of Roland the Matter of France, El Cid the Matter of Spain, and Barbarossa the Matter of Germany, so is the Alamo and all connected with it the Matter of Texas. In the early twentieth century, romantic novelists discovered that Travis, Bowie, Crockett, and Bonham made as good a story as did Lancelot, Bedivere, and the Lady of the Lake, and that ten inches of Arkansas-forged steel in Jim Bowie's hand could be as storied as Excalibur. They leaped head-on into the Matter of Texas.

A romantic novelist of the early 1930's achieved a not-too-successful blend of legends by constructing a tale in which Jim Bowie, Davy Crockett (who didn't even get to Texas until 1836), and other Texas heroes searched for the Lost San Saba Mine and found it to be the lost treasure of Moctezuma. Since Moctezuma's treasure is usually located (a) in a mysterious Aztec city hidden in a cavern below Mexico City, (b) in the Thunder God's house on Superstition Mountain in Arizona, (c) some where in the vastness of the Sierra Madre, or (d) in a volcanic cave in New Mexico's *malpaís*, it took quite a bit of imagination to transform it into the lost San Saba treasure, complete with Aztec guards wearing costumes left over from a road production of *Aïda*.

Paul I. Wellman, in his very successful biographical novel of James Bowie, *The Iron Mistress*, skirted the edges of the mine story while swallowing hook, line, and sinker the fictional account of Bowie's sojourn among the Lipans. The movie, starring Alan Ladd as Bowie, ended with Bowie's marriage to Ursula de Veramendi and left out the Indians and the silver mine.

It remained for a writer of pulp western fiction, Fran Striker, to give the silver mine its greatest notoriety. Striker created a character for a western magazine series: a Texas Ranger who was the only survivor of a patrol ambushed and wiped out by a band of outlaws. He adopted a domino mask as a disguise, and the Lone Ranger began a "never ending fight for justice in the Old West." As Striker's character developed, the writer gave him a distinctive trademark—he used bullets of pure silver. To explain the source of the silver slugs, Striker had the Lone Ranger's Indian companion reveal a tribal secret—an ancient Spanish silver mine, hidden deep in the Texas hills. It is interesting to note that the Lone Ranger's silver bullets coincide with the appearance of certain legends about the Lost San Saba Mine published in national-circulation magazines by a young but promising Texas writer who signed himself J. Frank Dobie.

Apparently Striker never tried to make a silver bullet to find out what was involved. In the 1960's the writing staff of a popular firearms magazine decided to experiment with silver bullets. They discovered that it takes a lot more to melt silver than an ordinary campfire. They wound up taking their silver to a manufacturing jeweler, since the equipment used to make ordinary lead bullets caused some very hot but otherwise unaffected silver. When the bullets were cast, a second discovery was made: silver bullets don't fall out of the mold ready to lubricate, size, and shoot. They must be dipped in an acid bath to remove surface irregularities. All in all, however, the report was favorable. Silver bullets are accurate, move at somewhat higher velocity than lead when driven by the same charge (they weigh considerably less than lead), and don't lose much metal when fired into sand. Still, they are expensive. The staff consensus was that while the Lone Ranger loaded some pretty good stuff, he went to a hell of a lot of trouble to make it.

In the 1960's Bridbooks, a British publisher of 1930's-style westerns, produced a novel (*The Hostile Plains*) several cuts above its customary mysterious-stranger-saves-the-heroine's-ranch, shoot-out-on-Main-Street, and six-shots-ahead-of-the-sheriff offerings. The subject was the Lost San Saba Mine, and the author, who goes by the name William H. Fear, had apparently done some homework, but he placed the treasure-trove of silver described in the 1866 *derrotero* produced by Carlota in the hands of the Caddos, who certainly never invaded Comanchería in the 1830's.

In 1975 James Wakefield Burke, a Texas writer, produced a massive novel entitled *The Blazing Dawn*, a new wave historical novel that paid much more attention to who was in whose bed than to its central theme, in this case the fall of the Alamo. Burke's research was spotty. In places it was impressively detailed, and in others—well, the name of Judge Robert McAlpin "Three-legged Willie" Williamson is available in any high school level Texas history text, so calling him William Williamson is unforgivable. Burke placed Jim Bowie, together with a caricature black named Sam and a character named Tex Delacey, in a cave full of silver bars near the old *presidio*. In fact, Bowie's servant, the one who was with him in 1831 when he supposedly found the "Lost Bowie Mine," was named Charles, and one would have to doubt the use of the nickname "Tex" before Texas became a republic.

The Lone Star Brewery in San Antonio maintains a Hall of Texas History, a walk-through series of dioramas, in HemisFair Plaza in San Antonio. One of the life-size scenes shows Jim Bowie at the Lost San Saba Mine and depicts Bowie in the company of the Lipan chief Xolic (who is wearing Sioux war regalia) examining a stack of silver bars in a cave complete with eerie lighting and animated bats.

The Lost San Saba Mine began mostly as a real estate promotion. Its continued existence in legend misdirected searchers and obscured Los Almagres for over a hundred years, and has, if anything, postponed serious attempts to hunt for mineral wealth in the Red Hills—and from all indications, there is a quite a bit to hunt.

CHAPTER VIII
Harp Perry and Los Almagres

The Mexican revolution 1810–1821 had a lot more effect on the history of the United States than most history books reveal. To begin with, we were more or less preoccupied with all sorts of interesting diversions of our own during the period. We had the war that gave us our national anthem and the Battle of New Orleans and produced a couple of presidents, the Aaron Burr–James Wilkinson manifest destiny scheme, and similar alarums and excursions. For these reasons and others, historians of the United States have tended to ignore the tremendous part that *norteamericanos*—mostly Yankees—played in the overthrow of the Spanish regime in Mexico. Mexican historians tend to ignore these same *norteamericanos* for reasons of national pride. Only in the history of Texas, and there very briefly, do you find them mentioned.

The part these *norteamericanos* played was a sacrificial one. They did not win a single major battle. They are honored with no statues, national holidays, or local celebrations. They did, however, tie up hundreds or even thousands of Spanish troops in east and central Texas and waste tons of war materiel that otherwise would have been used to great effect against the *revolutionistas* deep in Mexico. In a very real sense, Mexico owes its independence to these wildly opportunistic, totally self-committed filibusters, despite the fact that Mexico's independence was not what they had in mind. These were no high-minded freedom fighters. They were land-grabbing opportunists who were trying to take advantage of Spain's preoccupation and discomfiture in Mexico to carve personal empires out of the wilderness of Texas. Spain put them down easily, and in winning the battle, lost the war.

One of these expeditions, under the leadership of a Spanish-Mexican named Gutiérrez and a wild Irish-American named Magee, rode into northeast Texas under a green flag—the green of Ireland come to set up a new homeland in the new world, some said, determined to set up its own republic. In the ranks rode a young Yankee, scarcely more than a teenager. His name was Harper Perry, and beyond that we know practically nothing about him. All that we have is a story, first reported in a Galveston newspaper in the 1870's and later quoted almost verbatim in *Coronado's Children*, a half-forgotten story of how he died, and a weatherbeaten gravestone in an unkempt cemetery near Georgetown.

Harper Perry may be the most significant single figure of Anglo-American ancestry ever to be connected with the silver mine on the Llano. He's probably the one who took most of the silver out.

Gutiérrez and Magee, through incredible stupidity, came to grief near San Antonio. Their expedition was ambushed and virtually massacred, only a few escaping the general slaughter. The survivors split up and headed for the tall timber: some crept back across the Sabine into the United States; others, finding retreat to the east cut off, scattered. Two of them, one of whom was Perry, by accident or design, wound up heading southwest. Whether they figured the unknown dangers of the interior were less fearsome than an almost certain death by hanging or firing squad should they be caught by the Spanish regulars behind them, or whether they just plain got lost, we don't know. We do know that sometime around 1815 Perry and his unnamed partner turned up in San Antonio. There they apparently got wind of the silver prospects at Los Almagres and decided to take a look for themselves. They liked what they saw.

Perry and his partner were part of a long Texas tradition involving three rivers, the Río Grande, the Sabine, and the Red. They were illegal aliens whose feet were still wet with Sabine water. To admit they had found a workable silver vein at or near Los Almagres was to invite prison and loss. Illegal aliens who didn't make nuisances of themselves were generally ignored. Those who did something noteworthy—especially those who made money—drew all sorts of unpleasant attention. Mining, in particular, was subject to the king's fifth, and to mine without paying 20 percent into the royal treasury was a serious crime indeed.

Perry and partner disguised their operation as a farm. The tools to work a farm are, all considered, remarkably similar to those used to work a mine. Picks, shovels, axes, rakes, digging bars—all are useful in either operation. Only smelting equipment and explosives don't fit in with farming, and as for explosives, well, the only explosive in general use was gunpowder, and one would expect a farm or ranch in Indian country to use a lot of gunpowder. Besides, one could always use sotol heads, peon dynamite, to crack rock. The peons of Mexico had been using it for a couple of centuries. Holes were driven into the rock face. A fresh, moist head from a sotol stalk was forced into the hole, and the hole was tamped. A fire was built against the rock face. The fire heated the rock, which in turn heated the sotol head, causing the moisture in it to turn to steam. Expansion caused by the steam cracked the hot rock. It was simple, much less expensive, and considerably safer than using gunpowder. It took longer, but time was not as valuable as results.

Smelting requires three items that can't be disguised as much of anything. They are soapstone spoons for skimming slag and stirring chemicals into the melt, the chemicals themselves, and molds for bar metal. Soapstone spoons can be manufactured on site and apparently were. Chemicals can be mislabeled and disguised as medical supplies. Molds are just that—molds for molten metal. They don't look like anything else on earth except maybe cornbread pans, and only a total fool could be tricked into believing that. The importation or possession of molds is pretty much a dead giveaway that somebody is mining.

The Perry solution was not to use molds at all. All along the creek bottoms in the Red Hills there grew (and grow to this day) vast stands of a native cane. This cane doesn't produce anything of value, unlike sugar cane, and it is nowhere near as sturdy as bamboo. It has no apparent use, it would seem, except to produce canebrakes for animals and men to hide in, and to produce spears with which small boys play Indian. Perry found another use for it. When the cane is cut green and the partitions are knocked out of the hollow center, its moisture content is such that it is almost impossible to set the stuff afire. Molten silver could be poured into the cane without burning it away, and the silver would harden, long before the cane caught fire from its heat, into an unorthodox-looking but easily packed and carried silver bar. These silver "canes," once they have tarnished, look like nothing quite so much as a short piece of rebar or concrete reinforcing rod.

Perry and his partner may have started alone, but according to the story, before they had to abandon the mine they had upwards of twenty-five Mexican workers. They did start with the most logical step: they resmelted the old Spanish slagpile they found alongside the old smelter.

Spanish smelting methods in the eighteenth century, incidentally, were very wasteful. For years resmelting Spanish slag was a profitable occupation in Mexico, since the ancient smelting processes often left behind upwards of half the extractable silver. Indians in Mexico, as late as the early 1900's, dug into the old piles and found chunks of easily workable, almost pure silver. The resmelting of the slagpile would furnish a sizable stake for reopening the old mine, but where would the silver be sold? Certainly not in San Antonio—that would be suicide. How about New Orleans? The bars, carefully tarnished, could be passed off as lead or iron, and there were numerous silversmiths and a United States mint in New Orleans. If you have a piece of American-made silver or a silver coin made in New Orleans in the 1820's or early 1830's, it just may contain silver from the Lost San Saba Mine.

Silver was sold, tools were purchased, laborers were hired, and a mining operation of considerable extent was established at or near Los Almagres. According to the Perry story, ore was taken from several holes, the Los Almagres shaft being but one of them. This continued for about twenty years, coming to an abrupt end in 1834. Almost twenty years of continuous, albeit clandestine, mining requires that a lot of silver be sold somewhere to someone. Miners have to be paid, food has to be bought, chemicals and tools have to be replaced, and all the dozens of other incidental expenses of living have to be dealt with.

Then, in 1834, the axe fell on the Perry mining operation. The Comanches struck, killing every living soul except Perry, his partner, and the obligatory beautiful Mexican girl. When the smoke cleared, the partners surveyed the damage. All the laborers were dead. The tools, shelters, everything that would burn was in ashes. The smelter was destroyed, as was the ore crusher. To rebuild would be impossible without considerable help, and they could not afford to get help because of security. Money was no problem. They had better than twelve hundred pounds of silver canes ready for shipment—more than enough to re-establish the mine—but how would they go about it? They had no transport, since horses and mules were the first thing any Indian raid swallowed. They had no men, and they couldn't very well walk into San Antonio and start hiring. To go to the Mexican governor's office in San Antonio and say something like, "Hey, Governor, we've been stealing silver out of a mine up on the Llano for the last twenty years or so and selling it in New Orleans, but the Comanches burned us out so we'd like to sell you some silver so we can buy equipment and hire men to re-start the mine so we can steal some more" would not be, all considered, a move of the greatest perspicacity.

Each partner took as much silver as he could carry and the rest, some twelve hundred pounds, was buried "on a high hill about a half mile north of the old smelter." Then the three set out for St. Louis, where the partner married the girl and opened a saloon. Perry dropped out of sight for more than thirty years.

In 1866 a grizzled, hardfaced old man rode into San Antonio. His name, he said, was Harp Perry, and he had a story. The story was about silver—a rich silver mine on the Llano, and a treasure-trove of twelve hundred pounds of bar silver to go with it. He needed help in finding it. He was hunting for the old Spanish smelter, and he had $500 in Yankee gold for the man who could lead him to it.

Perry wanted—and this is important—not the mine, but the twelve hundred pounds of bar silver. Never once did he mention reopening the old mine. Why not? My guess is that he was fully aware that he and his partner, in twenty years or so of mining, had exhausted the resources of Miranda's Cueva de San José del Alcazar. The item of real value on the Llano at that time was not the Lost San Saba Mine itself, but Perry's silver cache.

Even for $500, a fortune in itself in Reconstruction Texas, Perry found no takers. The Red Hills, save for the German enclaves around Fredericksburg, were Comanchería as never before. It would be ten long and bloody years before the last Indian fight took place on the slopes of Packsaddle Mountain, only about three miles east of the Los Almagres stope. The men of San Antonio were brave, but they were not foolish. No one rode with Harp Perry into the Red Hills.

Perry, however, was desperate enough to go alone. He made several trips into the hills, using San Antonio as a base. Thirty years, he found, is a very long time. What had been open land was covered with brush. Where stands of timber had been, fire had left barrens. Memory played dirty tricks with landmarks. The hills had changed, and Harp Perry never found his old smelter, and without it as a landmark, he could not ride to the cache of silver bars.

In the spring of 1867, discouraged and nearly broke, Harp Perry decided to go to St. Louis, locate his old partner, and return to the hills for one final search. He joined a trail drive making for Missouri, and a week later, at a campsite in Williamson County near Georgetown, he died in a freakish but fairly common accident. It took me ten years to find out what happened.

Harp Perry was an unadulterated fool. He carried a Colt six-shooter, and he carried the thing fully loaded with the hammer down on a loaded and capped chamber. He was saddling his horse, getting ready to move out. He threw the saddle on the animal, hooked the near-side stirrup over the horn, and cinched the saddle tight. He then unhooked the stirrup and let it fall.

It's a natural action; I've done it myself, hundreds of times. So has anyone else who ever regularly saddled and unsaddled a horse. I'm still alive. So are most of the others who have done it—or at least they didn't die of a dropped stirrup. But then, I wasn't and they weren't wearing a Colt six-shooter with the hammer down on a capped nipple in an open-topped holster that was directly in the line of the stirrup's fall. It takes three pounds of pressure, suddenly applied, to fire a percussion cap. The stirrup, striking the revolver's hammer after falling more than a foot, generated appreciably more than three pounds of impact energy. The revolver discharged; the ball entered Perry's right leg just above the knee and smashed into the artery. He bled to death in about fifteen minutes. He's buried in a neglected grave in an obscure cemetery in Williamson County.

So ends the story of Harper Perry. Legend, nothing more. No concrete proof. Or is there?

In August 1979, I met a most remarkable man. His name is D. B. Mull. He lives, every now and then, in Geronimo, Texas. He describes himself as a bum. He too has hunted, from time to time, the elusive silver of the Red Hills.

"I once found some real peculiar silver bars up near Llano," he said. "Found 'em in a creek bottom. Looked like somebody had dropped them while they were carrying a bunch of them someplace. They were about a foot, maybe a foot and a half long, about an inch or so in diameter. Round, with funny marks on 'em. Looked like they had been molded inside a piece of cane."

"Mr. Mull," I asked, "does the name Harp Perry mean anything to you?"

He scratched the gray flattop he wears. "No," he said, finally, "can't say I've ever heard of the feller. Why?"

CHAPTER IX
Jim Bowie and the Lost Bowie Mine

The evidence that
Bowie brothers Jim and Rezin P had
anything at all to do with a mine of any
sort anywhere is tenuous, being mostly

rumor and legend, but then, the evidence for silver mines themselves isn't much more conclusive. There is, however, one piece of good, hard—rock hard, you might say—evidence that someone named Bowie had something to do with a mine somewhere around the old Presidio San Saba. In the ruins of the old fort, on one of the gateposts, you can find the words BOWIE MINE and the date 1832 carved into the stone. If that inscription is genuine, then either Jim or Rezin P Bowie carved it there and it means something.

Well, the inscription is real—or at least part of it is. Well into the 1920's, after the Indians were driven out of central Texas, but before barbed wire cut up the range, the old Presidio San Saba ruins were a popular picnic spot for church and family groups and a lovers' trysting place. An inscription that read BOWIE CON SU TROPA 1829 was known on the site.

It is fairly safe to assume that James Bowie *con su tropa* ("with his men") was in the area of the old *presidio* as early as 1829, and that Bowie, needing a campsite he could defend if necessary, used the old *presidio*, probably more than once. The urge to manufacture graffiti is deep within the human psyche, and probably as old as writing. An inscription on a wall in Pompeii informs us, some two thousand years after the fact, that "Marcus has the ears of a jackass." While that one is hardly significant, graffiti are sometimes of great historical value. In the 1500's, a Portuguese named Miguel Cortereal left his name and a date on Dighton Rock, thus providing us with a clue to one of the earliest penetrations by white men into what is now New England. Juan de Oñate left his name and the date 1661 on Inscription Rock, thus providing an important piece of information about the extent of Spanish exploration in the Southwest. A young surveyor named George Washington carved his initials into the rock at Natural Bridge, Virginia, and an illiterate long hunter named Dan Boone recorded on a tree in Kentucky the fact that D BOON CILLD A BAR ON TREE together with the date. In like manner, Jim Bowie or just possibly Rezin P took a piece of iron or a sharp rock and recorded the passage of Bowie *con su tropa* on the gatepost of the old *presidio* in 1829.

The inscription remained untouched for many years, and small boys delighted in poking around in the weeds to find it and point it out to incredulous friends, relatives, and new-comers, while their concerned parents undoubtedly called, "Come away from there, you young fool, before you stir up a rattler." It remained untouched until, sometime between 1895 and 1910, a nameless vandal with a better than average knowl-edge of Texas history and legend obliterated CON SU TROPA 1829, and left the inscription reading BOWIE MINE 1832. In addi-tion to destroying an important piece of Texas history, he spread confusion among several generations of Texans.

Before we go any further, let's get something on record. James Bowie—the Colonel Jim Bowie of Bowie knife and Alamo fame, the man responsible for the second most famous name of the Lost San Saba Mine, the Lost Bowie Mine—certainly never worked, probably never saw, and in all likelihood never even looked for the Lost San Saba or any other silver mine.

We have seen that Perry, who worked the Cueva de San José del Alcazar, the original Los Almagres silver strike, mined silver for about twenty years, abandoning the mine in 1834. Bowie entered Texas for the first time—legally—while Perry and his partner were mining, before they were driven away from Los Almagres by the Comanches.

Jim and Rezin P Bowie were land speculators, and their business practices would probably get their licenses jerked by the Texas Real Estate Commission today. Their business was to find suckers and sell them land in Indian country, and they were good at it. They did, however, need capital, if only to grease the slow-turning wheels of Mexican bureaucracy. Part of their prob-lem with the bureaucracy was solved when Jim married the vice-governor's daughter—a marriage that might well have involved

love but was by no means politically or financially disadvan-
tageous—but money was even more helpful. And the Bowie
brothers produced their assets in the form of bar silver, which
they allegedly got from a secret Indian silver mine in the Red
Hills. According to the Bowies, Jim lived with the Lipans for a
time and was shown the mine after demonstrating his disdain
for silver by presenting Xolic, chief of the Lipans, with an
elaborate silver-mounted rifle.

This story has more holes than a colander. To begin with,
the Lipans were not a Red Hills tribe. By 1800 the Red Hills were
pretty solidly Comanchería, with occasional timid incursions by
the Tonkawas from the east and bolder forays by the Apaches
from beyond the Pecos. And Bowie's movements from the time
he legally entered Texas until he died in the Alamo are fairly
well documented. There isn't a two- or three-year gap for Bowie
to drop out of sight and become "an Indian in all but color."

There was, however, someone who did fill the bill. Caiphas
(Cephas) K. Ham, another Texican and a sometime companion
of the Bowies, did in fact live with the Indians, the Comanches,
for about two years. According to Ham, a fat warrior who was
his best friend among the Indians once pointed out a red hill
and said, "Other side, plenty silver," or words to that effect.
With the exception of the silver-mounted rifle and being shown
the actual mine, the Bowie yarn almost exactly, and very suspiciously, parallels Ham's story. However, there remains to be
explained the bar silver the Bowies did show up with on numerous occasions. It was real, and it was spent by the Bowies in San
Antonio.

There is a persistent legend that the Mexican government
sent mule trains of silver bars overland from the mines of
Sonora to New Orleans and perhaps other points in the United
States. These silver caravans consisted of one hundred to three
hundred mules, each loaded with six fifty-pound bars of pure
silver. As with most Spanish and Mexican ventures of this sort,

the caravans were undermanned and underguarded. A typical force accompanying a 300-mule train might well consist of a half-dozen unarmed muleskinners, three or four musket-armed soldiers, and a sergeant or a junior officer in charge. It would seem, at first glance, that the soldiers would have no trouble organizing a mutiny, taking the silver, and heading for the States, but in fact the sergeant in charge usually carried all the ammunition, issuing powder and ball to the soldiers only when danger threatened. The sergeant would be armed, of course, usually with a sword and a brace of flintlock pistols.

This was only incidentally an antimutiny measure. Mexican soldiers were poorly, and seldom, paid. For years they used gunpowder as a substitute for money, trading portions of their issue powder charges for food, liquor, or female favors every time they got to a town, the hand-rolled paper *cartucho* being refilled with sand to deceive an inspector. The problem continued into the twentieth century, until the Mexican army traded the last of its black powder rifles for smokeless powder ones.

The silver trail entered Texas at what is now Presidio, old Presidio del Norte on the Río Bravo; it then snaked through the mountains, crossed the Pecos at Horsehead Crossing, and angled southeast along the general route followed today by IH-10/US 290 to San Antonio, where it joined the Old Spanish Trail, El Camino Real, across east Texas, winding up eventually at Natchitoches, Louisiana, on the Red River, about ten miles east of old Los Adaes. It was a long road, and by no means was most of it peaceful. A dozen or fewer men, only half or so armed, weren't going to put up much of a fight against anyone, red or white. They also weren't too likely to stay spread out along the long train. More likely, they all stayed close to the lead mule and let the end of the train worry about itself.

Even those small Spanish mules occupied a good bit of linear space. It was a minimum of three yards, sometimes as much as four, from the nose of one mule to the nose of the one behind. A 100-mule column stretched between three and four hundred yards, and a 300-mule train was considerably more than a half-mile long. The mules were linked by ropes, and where the lead mule went the trail mule would, eventually, follow, usually at a slow walk. It could easily take a month, perhaps longer, to walk mules from Presidio to San Antonio, and there were no real checkpoints in between. Three hundred mules would carry over a million troy ounces of pure silver, all guarded by three or four men with unloaded muskets and one man with a dull sword and a pair of unreliable flintlock pistols.

As the mule train wound in and out of the brush and through the hills, more often than not several trail mules were out of sight of the lead mule and thus out of sight of the guard. It wouldn't have been difficult for a daring man with a sharp knife to hide alongside the trail, wait until the last three or four mules passed by, and then cut the line and head for parts unknown with nine hundred to twelve hundred pounds of bar silver. By the time the loss was discovered, several hours and a few miles down the trail, nobody could be quite sure where and when the mules disappeared. More important, at least from the thief's point of view, no one was overly anxious to go back and find out.

A man in possession of three or four mules loaded with silver, especially if he had a lot of political pull, a reasonably plausible story, and a reputation as a bad man to tangle with, just might go unquestioned. James Bowie, Don Diego Bowie, El Cuchillo Grande, the man with the big, mean-looking knife and the reputation to go with it, who also happened to be the son-in-law of the vice-governor of Coahuila and Texas and had already claimed to know the whereabouts of a silver mine in the hills, filled the bill exactly.

This much is speculation. There is no documentary evidence, so far as I know, that Jim Bowie did in fact steal his bar silver from the Mexican government. There is, however, a lot of circumstantial evidence.

First, of course, is the matter of Bowie's tale of living with the Lipans. Between the Vidalia sandbar fight and the death of Ursula de Veramendi Bowie there simply isn't enough time not otherwise accounted for to substantiate the alleged sojourn among the Indians. Bowie did "drop out of sight" for two years after his wife's death—into the gutters of San Antonio, where he was known as El Borracho Grande—but all the bar silver showed up *before* Ursula died.

Bowie, we think, had been in Texas before. There is an undocumented story that the Bowies traded slaves with the Lafittes and others in the early 1800's, but while the story may be true it has never been proved. It is quite true that Jim Bowie was a reckless youngster, and there are a lot of gaps in this part of his life, but it seems unlikely that he took off across Spanish Texas to find a band of Indians he'd probably never heard of on the off chance they'd adopt him (instead of killing him out of hand) and show him a silver mine.

There is the remarkable similarity between the Bowie story and Caiphas K. Ham's tale. Ham did, in fact, live with the Comanches. He did roam the Red Hills in their company. He was a friend and sometime business associate of the Bowies. He was known as a storyteller, and he undoubtedly spun his yarn for Jim and Rezin P.

Then there's the joker in the deck. The Bowies had bar silver, and they got it somewhere. Where?

One of the more famous frontiersman-Indian scraps in pre-revolution Texas was the November 1831 "Battle of Calf Creek." James Bowie, his brother Rezin P, and, depending on who's doing the telling, somewhere between fourteen and twenty-five men including a black cook tangled with a band of Indians, somewhere between one hundred fifty and two hundred in number, variously described as Comanches, Lipans, or a composite band of Wacos and Tawakonis. The fight took place somewhere along the San Saba River, east of the old *presidio* at Menard and west of Brady.

Exactly where this fight occurred is a matter for debate. There are almost as many sites for the battle as there are tellers for the tale. The state of Texas considers a location along the San Saba tributary called Calf Creek, south and slightly west of Brady in McCulloch County, as correct—hence the name—and has erected a Texas Historical Marker to that effect. Rezin P Bowie, who was there, said the fight took place "six miles east of the old fort" at a site generally conceded to be Jackson's Creek, just east of Menard. Certain silver seekers in Menard County will tell you that it took place at Silver Creek, nine miles west and about three miles north of the old *presidio*. Another source suggests, not without reason, a dry wash once known as Turkey Creek. Alongside both Calf Creek and Jackson's Creek there were, at one time, rough rings of rock and downed timber that suggested hastily erected breastworks. Both were known locally as "Bowie's Fort."

There's almost as much controversy over what happened as there is over where it happened. One of the more romantic stories has it that the "gallant Frontiersmen" held off the "painted devils" in a siege lasting anywhere from three days to a week. Rezin P Bowie said it was an all-day fight, and Bowie—followed closely by Wellman in *The Iron Mistress*—told it as a sort of Texican version of Beecher's Island, with volley after volley of rifle fire repulsing charge after charge until the ground was littered with copper-skinned corpses and gore. Most historical accounts tend to follow this pretty closely, setting the Indian losses at 30 to 50 percent in front of the Texican rifles. There were either two or three casualties inside the breastwork, and only one of those, Tom McCaslin, has ever been reported as killed. No one asked the Indians how many they lost.

One of the wounded was Matthew A. Doyal. He's called

Matt Doyle in both Wellman's and Burke's novels, and his name, spelled incorrectly, is on the Calf Creek monument. He told his children and grandchildren a somewhat different story of the fight, and one of his grandsons, Ralph A. Doyal, told it to me. It differs radically from the accepted version.

The purpose of the expedition, according to Matt Doyal, was not to hunt for a lost mine, scout for Indians, examine land, explore the country, or any of the other reasons given by historians, but rather to steal three or four mules from a Mexican silver train.

Historians have made much of the fact that the Bowie party was "out of sight" for almost twenty days between leaving San Antonio and turning up on Calf Creek, which is at most a five-day march. Dobie even went so far as to speculate that Bowie might have been digging in more than one mine in that time. According to Doyal, who was there, most of the time was spent holed up in the brush waiting for a scheduled silver train to pass a pre-selected ambush point somewhere west of present-day Junction.

The ambush was not a fusillade of rifle fire from the brush, followed by an unheralded mass burial among the rocks. There is a rumor that Bowie once got greedy and snatched a whole train but that was not the plan this time. This ambush was to be the careful theft of the last three or four mules and their silver packs without the guards knowing until it was too late.

According to Doyal, the men seized three mules. At this point the story used to break down. Americans, inured to generations of artificially depressed silver prices (as low as $1.25 an ounce, and don't you wish you'd bought silver bullion in 1950?) could not understand why Bowie bothered with a mere $12,000 worth of silver to be divided so many ways.

Each mule carried six fifty-pound bars of pure silver. Three hundred pounds of silver is 3,600 troy ounces. Three mules carried 900 pounds—10,800 troy ounces. At $12 an ounce, 10,800 troy ounces of pure silver works out to $129,600. Divided four-teen ways—the cook, being a slave, could not legally hold property—it works out to $9,250 and some pennies per man. More than 771 ounces of silver, in 1832, and for almost all time, except when our silver prices were artificially low, was a fair stake anywhere.

When Bowie and his party snatched the mules they set out in a generally northwesterly direction to lay a false trail into Indian country and deceive any half-hearted pursuit. Then they planned to swing east, march into the Red Hills, and enter San Antonio from the north, which would make it appear that they had come from the vicinity of Packsaddle Mountain, the direction in which legend insisted the mine lay.

Doyal's account of the fight is nowhere near so glamorous as the Bowie version, and under careful scrutiny the Bowie account tends to fall apart at the seams. A Beecher's Island type fight with flintlock single-shot rifles and pistols, even 25 Tex-icans (the largest number anyone has allotted) to 150 Indians (the smallest number mentioned), just doesn't hold up.

The US Cavalry at Beecher's Island broke the charges of Roman Nose by doing their best to burn the barrels off their seven-shot Spencer repeaters, and they had a six-shooter apiece for backup. A good man with a Spencer could throw out seven well-directed if not perfectly aimed .50-caliber slugs in about twenty-five seconds, take about thirty-five seconds to reload, and then do it again, and he could keep doing it until the barrel got hot enough to cook off the cartridges as they were chambered, or until one of the myriad other ills to which the Spencer was subject caused him to pull out his pocket knife and repair the thing.

A real expert with a flintlock plains rifle, and we are fairly sure most of the rifles at Calf Creek were flintlock, using pre-measured powder charges, pregreased patches, and balls pre-positioned in a loading block, can, if he's both very good and very lucky, start with a loaded rifle and get off about three aimed shots in, say, a minute and a half. Call it eighty seconds to be charitable. That presupposes ideal conditions: he's standing up to load and fire, everything is neatly laid out on a table-top or a flat rock at waist height, the ramrod is out of the pipes and it doesn't break, and he doesn't drop anything. Lying flat on your belly in the grama grass and shooting over a rock or a log, then reloading while lying flat on your back, all while someone is doing his determined best to kill you and musket balls are plunking into logs or ricocheting off rocks within inches of your head does not qualify as ideal conditions.

If we assume the Indians were at minimum strength, 150 minus 15 horseholders, and the white men numbered 25, each with a rifle and a pistol, and the Indians charged from 100 yards (maximum approach time about twenty seconds), and all the rifles and pistols actually fired and nobody missed even once, we are still left with 85 Indians going nose to nose with 25 white men after the shooting is over. Bowie's ground littered with dead Indians and charge after charge broken just won't wash.

The battle, according to Doyal, wasn't all that much of a contest. There were three or four really expert riflemen among the Texicans, and every time the Indians got ready to rush the breastwork they would pick off the leaders. This led to a number of long "who's gonna lead the next one" discussions among the Indians, and they never actually charged the white men at all. The only Indian who got close enough to do any damage crept up to the breastwork through the tall grass, poked a large-caliber musket through the gaps, and let fly. The first shot chipped a man's shin. The second hit Doyal in the chest. The third time he tried it, one Texican grabbed the musket barrel, yanked, and shoved down. As the astonished warrior's head popped up over the low breastwork, a second Texican took dead aim with a buckshot-loaded horse-pistol. Indian casualties probably totaled less than a dozen.

When night fell the Indians pulled back, taking all the party's horses and mules but not the silver. The silver packs were part of the breastwork. The Bowie party knew they were in a very vulnerable position, and if they were foolish enough to be there when the sun rose they would probably be there permanently. First, they didn't have the food, ammunition, or water to withstand a siege. They were too weak and too badly outnumbered to make anything but a last stand, and if there is a viable alternative, last stands aren't all that appealing. Second, they had two wounded men, both of whom were litter cases. Leaving them behind was not open to consideration. Third, there was the 900 pounds of silver. A fifty-pound bar of silver isn't a convenient size to mount on your shoulder and balance while carrying. The old Spanish and Mexican two-arroba bars measure about 6″ x 3½″ x 3″, a size which will fit conveniently into a pants pocket but would be somewhat disconcerting to carry that way, especially if your pants or your suspenders were a little weak. Of the fifteen available men, only nine could be carrying silver at any one time, the other six being engaged in carrying or lying on litters. Packing a hundred pounds of silver in your britches has to be just about twice as much trouble as packing fifty. Making swift and silent progress over unfamiliar ground at night is hard enough when you're unencumbered.

They decided to bury the silver, and while we may trust Doyal's account of the fight, his version of the treasure-hole may be open to some doubt. The man had, after all, taken a large-caliber musket ball—most trade muskets were either .69 or .75 caliber, or about ¾ of an inch in diameter—in the chest. His attention had to be divided, to say the least.

The silver was buried waist deep "on a tall man," about three feet, in a hole dug in the immediate vicinity of the breastwork. The frontiersmen, yielding to that strange impulse that tends to cause treasure-buriers to bury something personal with the treasure-trove, put in a knife described as a Bowie and a tomahawk. The hole was refilled and thoroughly tamped, and then marked so it could be found again. The marks were three "Injun rocks" (probably flints) of roughly triangular shape, buried in a triangle, their points toward the cache. The rocks were dug into the ground so that they appeared to be natural. This done, the entire party, including the cook, swore never to return to the silver unless all were present.

Once the treasure was concealed, a pair of litters were built and the party set out afoot, traveling east downstream on the San Saba. Those who hold that Tom McCaslin was killed during the fight insist that he, too, was buried, a short distance from the breastwork, and that his grave was marked in some manner. Doyal and the other man were left to recover at a settlement near present Camp San Saba, south of Brady, and the rest straggled back into San Antonio with a harrowing tale of an Indian fight on the San Saba.

The following spring an epidemic of Yellow Jack struck San Antonio. Bowie sent his wife and child to Monclova to stay with relatives in hopes of avoiding it. But then, Yellow Jack struck Monclova, killing the beautiful Ursula and James Bowie's only known descendant. El Cuchillo Grande became El Borracho Grande, and although there is rumor that he went back to the hills, there is no record of it.

Whether or not you accept this story will depend on whether or not you accept that the silver trains did, in fact, exist. A pretty good case can be made, using available historical documentation, or the lack of it, that they didn't. An equally good case can be made, based on what we know about the economy of Mexico in the early and mid-nineteenth century, that they— or something very like them—had to exist.

Granted that the silver trains are undocumented, how did Mexico pay for what it bought? There were practically no manufacturing facilities in Mexico until the mid-twentieth century. Spain permitted none—Mexico supplied raw materials, most notably precious metal, and Spain provided manufactured goods, generally at greatly inflated prices.

Between 1821, the year Mexico won its independence from Spain, and 1836, when Texas forcibly dissociated itself from Mexico, and for many years thereafter, the Mexican government was notoriously unstable. In one eighteen-month period Mexico had nineteen governments, at least one of which lasted less than an hour and several of which lasted only a few days, all but the last being removed by gunfire rather than constitutional means. This sort of governmental instability does very little to boost international confidence in a nation's credit rating. One regime might order, say, 5,000 cavalry sabers from a jobber in Germany and issue a promissory note to pay on delivery. By the time the sabers were delivered and the promissory note was presented for payment, the government might well have changed seven or eight times, the note having been declared null and void by any number of people, and everyone connected with the original order might well be dead, exiled, or imprisoned. It was not, in fact, until the regime of Porfirio Díaz that Mexico had a government and economy stable enough to allow it to buy on credit.

Yet Mexico bought, and bought extensively, in both Europe and the United States. In Santa Anna's army of 1836, virtually everything that was manufactured, from the shakos on the *soldados'* heads to the refined opium the *generalísimo* kept in the silver-lined compartment in the hollow horn of his elaborate saddle, was bought in Europe or the States. Even the gunpowder that loaded the army's *escopetas* was imported. And speaking of muskets, Santa Anna may have admired Napoleon Bonaparte, but apparently he had no qualms about dealing with those who vanquished his idol. The Mexican *escopeta* was, in fact, more likely to be a British-made, Napoleonic War surplus Enfield Long Land Model musket, a Brown Bess, than anything else.

All of this had to be paid for, and we may be assured it was paid for in hard cash—metal, not paper. Coinage, however, was no more to be trusted than paper. Coins can be debased (alloyed with base metal), trimmed, or overvalued. Bullion can be tested for purity and the value assessed almost immediately. One thing Mexico had plenty of was silver, and it was easier to mold fifty-pound bars of pure silver than it was to turn out silver coins one at a time on a screw press.

Shipping silver by sea was risky, however. Mexico had a small navy and practically no international merchant marine. Bars had to be loaded on foreign sail, and that was dangerous. Not only were there pirates and the normal perils of the sea, but also the danger of mutiny ending with the crew splitting the silver and settling into retirement half a world away, or the captain embezzling the bullion and doing the same.

The solution was to transfer large quantities of bullion to a nearby nation that had a stable government and wasn't likely to freeze assets or nationalize banks. The closest nation to fill the bill was the United States; the closest banks were those in New Orleans.

There were numerous roads across Texas, most of which met at Bexar (San Antonio). From there one road in particular lead eastward, the old Camino Real or Royal Road, today marked on Texas maps as the Old Spanish Road or Old Spanish Trail. While bandits existed on practically every other road, the Camino Real had always been singularly free of road agents, a legacy of the road's royal status, when crimes committed elsewhere were merely crimes, but crimes committed on the Camino Real were crimes against the Crown and punished accordingly.

El Camino Real meandered across east Texas, through the Neutral Strip—which, by the 1830's, no longer existed except as a concept—and into Louisiana, terminating at old Los Adaes. Los Adaes had long since gone to ruin, but the road hadn't; it was, and remained for many years afterward, the only decent road in western Louisiana. It had been extended for about twelve miles into Natchitoches, which was then a major port on the Red River. From Natchitoches, where the pack animals were sold, it was a leisurely float down to the Mississippi and on to New Orleans, where the bullion was deposited and good-as-gold bankers' letters of credit were issued. With these Mexico could buy anything, anywhere, and regardless of the vagaries of dictators and firing squads, the vendors were assured of being able to claim hard cash or bullion in payment.

There is an interesting postscript. During the weeks preceding the Battle of the Alamo, Jim Bowie and his mounted volunteers had the job of scouting the area around San Antonio. On one of his forays Bowie spotted a long train of pack mules guarded by Mexican soldiers. The packs, he told his men, were loaded with enough silver to finance the whole revolution. The volunteers went after the train in a headlong charge. The soldiers immediately abandoned their posts and headed for the tall timber, leaving Bowie and the Texicans in undisputed possession of a mule train loaded with—hay. The mules carried packs laden with prairie grass, cut as fodder for the Mexican cavalry's horses. This incident, known to history as the Grass Fight, becomes very significant in light of Matt Doyal's story.

CHAPTER X

The Mine That Was on the San Saba
All the Time

Go get a piece of string and a Texas highway map. Using the mile scale in the map legend, tie a knot in your string, measure seventy leagues—210 miles—and tie another knot. Place one knot on the star in the center of San Antonio and with the other swing a seventy-league arc, northwest to northeast. It will enclose San Angelo and touch Cisco and Hillsboro. Now reduce the length of your string by a third. We have been dealing with airplane leagues. We need to deal with muleback leagues. Swing another arc. You will find that it passes almost exactly halfway between Eden and Menard, just about at the Menard County line.

Now listen to Don Ignacio Obregón, a Spaniard who signed himself "Royal Inspector of Mines" in the year of our Lord 1812: "The Almagres mine was found by accident, and is situated about seventy leagues north of San Antonio de Bexar. The specimens of ore that I send with this report were taken from near the surface, in my presence, and will show the exceeding wealth of this mine, which, according to analysis made here by Padre Anselmo, yields as high as 30 marks to the *carga* and is found in *bolsillos* ["pockets"]. That taken out is in the form of iguanas [literally, large lizard-sized chunks], some weighing as much as one-fourth of a quintal [about twenty-five pounds] and almost in a pure state. The geological formations of this region are of *la naturaleza de piedra calliza* ["limestone"], and the mineralogist would not for a moment suspect such a rich deposit of silver as exists in this vicinity."

Menard lies about seventy overland leagues north and slightly west of San Antonio. The formations in Menard County are limestone, and as I have been very careful to point out, nobody in his right mind would ever look twice at Menard County if he was hunting for silver. That would be a mistake. There is silver in Menard County. Good paying ore has been taken out by geologists in the twentieth century. It is against all reason, I agree, but gold is where you find it, and so, it would seem, is silver.

How long did the mine at Menard operate? We don't know. In 1758 Ortiz Parilla requested that his garrison and *presidio* be pulled back to the Río de las Chanas to protect the minerals there, which "if worked. . . ." The Los Almagres minerals—the real Los Almagres minerals, down on the Llano—weren't being worked in 1758. Neither were the Menard minerals, at least one source of which lies three leagues west and about a league north of the *presidio*. They certainly weren't being worked in 1769, when Don Felipe de Rabago y Teran was relieved of command for the second time and the Real Presidio de San Saba was officially abandoned.

In 1810 one Teniente Padilla and an apparent civilian named José María García visited the old *presidio*. They commented that silver was lying almost on the surface and recommended that the old fort be regarrisoned and the mine worked.

That same year in Dolores, deep in the Mexican interior, a priest called Padre Hidalgo rang a bell and raised a *grito*, a shout that had been sweeping the world—*Libertad! Libertad!* Liberty! Liberty! Although no one knew it at the time, it was the beginning of the end for Spain in Mexico and the death knell for all mining operations conducted officially in Texas. By 1812, when Obregón made his report, the gnat that was the revolution had become a pesky mosquito. The rich mining operation on the San Saba was doomed.

In 1821 Mexico became an independent nation. The mine on the San Saba was already closed, and the records of the operation concealed, destroyed, or transported out of the country. Only a few cryptic references remained, and most of them were thought to refer to the real Los Almagres, the red dirt hole in Cerro del Almagre, down on Honey Creek in Llano County. The possibility that there might be silver or anything else in Menard County didn't really occur to anyone again until 1866—anyone except the citizens of Menard. To them, Menard was and is the home of the Lost Jim Bowie/Lost San Saba Mine, and that's all there is to that.

Old-timers in Menard today point proudly to the BOWIE

MINE 1832 inscription on the gatepost at the old *presidio* to "prove" that Jim Bowie worked "their" silver mine—but the folks who were old-timers when these old-timers were still playing "Jim Bowie an' the Injuns" with wooden guns knew a different Bowie inscription on the gatepost. Those old-timers, though, had what they believed was a more positive indication of silver on the San Saba. Before the state of Texas used the centennial year of 1936 to reconstruct the ruins of Real Presidio de San Saba to a state of "arrested decay," there was, near the north wall, an old smelter. At least it was called a smelter. Dr. von Roemer, who went over the ruins pretty carefully in the 1840's, didn't mention it, and J. Frank Dobie speculated that the German doctor was too astute and sophisticated a student of antiquities to mistake the burnt rocks in a kitchen midden for a mineral smelter.

Be that as it may, the rock walls of the old fort provide a better break against the bitter north winds that sweep down from the high plains, and better protection against Comanche bullets and arrows, than does a motte of liveoaks. If there was a silver smelter in Menard County, there is no better place for it than adjacent to the ruined fort. One might ask, however, based on Obregón's description of the ore as *plata pura*, what purpose a smelter served. You don't have to reduce 90 percent pure silver—US sterling is only 92 percent pure.

Smelter or no, back in the days when Menard was a frontier outpost and men who plowed fields plowed small ones, a clear trail led from the burnt rocks against the *presidio's* north wall across the prairie to the northwest. It terminated in the vicinity of what is now called the "silver mine," and all around the area there were clear indications that someone had, for years, been making charcoal from the native oaks. Since it is doubtful that the Indians, the Spaniards, or Jim Bowie charbroiled their venison and buffalo steaks, the charcoal had to have another purpose.

There are three good uses for charcoal. You can use it in Satan's Trinity—sulfur, saltpeter, and charcoal—to make gunpowder. You can pour raw whiskey through it to take off the "bardy grease" (fusel oil) and make the stuff fit for human consumption. Or, you can use it to produce a hot fire for blacksmithing, melting lead to make bullets, or smelting ore.

Ask who did all this, and you'll be told "Jim Bowie—who else?" Ask who worked the mine, and again you'll be told "Jim Bowie—who else?" Ask where Bowie fought the Indians in November 1831 (the Calf Creek Fight), and you'll be directed to Silver Creek and to what is supposedly Tom McCaslin's grave. Doubt it—openly—and keep your guard up. Menard loves Jim Bowie, and casting doubts upon his accomplishments there, whether real or fictional, is not healthy.

James Bowie never worked the diggings near Menard. They were worked before, and after, his time. He was there, never doubt that, but not to dig silver.

The Spaniards probably closed and thoroughly concealed those holes sometime between 1815 and 1818, when Jim Bowie was still sawing logs in Louisiana and trading slaves with the Lafitte brothers. Having closed the mines, they moved south and destroyed or concealed the records. This was probably done to prevent the Mexican revolutionaries from seizing the rich mine and using the silver to finance their revolution even more thoroughly. Finally, in 1821, Spain lost the war and Mexico became an independent nation. The Menard diggings were, truly, the "Lost Mine on the San Saba," and they have as much or more right to be called the "Lost San Saba Mine" as Miranda's better known prospect on Honey Creek.

They were not, however, so widely publicized. Desultory digging has gone on around the old *presidio* for as long as there have been Anglo settlers in the Menard area—the "Spanish Gold" syndrome that affects all areas upon which Spanish feet have ever trodden—but nobody versed in geology or even in

115

legend took seriously the idea that there might be silver in the limestone near Menard until after the War between the States.

Four men began this story. Their names were Dixon, Sam Fleming, G. B. Ezell, and Wiley Stroud. They had a chart, a *derrotero*, to the location of a mine tunnel containing 2,000 bars of silver that was three leagues west of the old *presidio* and one league north of the San Saba River up a tributary known as Silver Creek. The *derrotero* mentioned fourteen mines around the abandoned fort, some as far as six leagues (eighteen miles) away, the richest of which was called Las Iguanas. The 2,000 bars of silver were said to be located in the main tunnel of the Las Iguanas Mine.

This *derrotero* came from the great cathedral at Monclova, from which it was stolen by a Mexican woman named Carlota. There seemed to be no doubt that it was genuine. It called first for landmarks, and then for hidden clues, among them a broken *metate* or corn-grinding stone, six copper pegs buried at intervals of thirty *varas*, and a three-forked oak tree with a flint rock the size of a turkey's egg buried in the forks.

All of the landmarks were found, and the hidden clues proved to be right where the *derrotero* said they should be, a feature not often found in treasure-map stories. The copper pegs were heavily corroded and the flint rock was deeply ingrown in the oak tree. An intersection was found, and the *metate*, which was marked with the word EXCAVAD ("dig") indicated that there would be some digging involved. It would be necessary, so the *derrotero* said, to clean out a large hole some seventy feet deep, and then some long and twisting tunnels. It was a major project. Ultimately the four men, all from San Marcos, quit, after putting down a pretty fair hole. They left the area forever.

Early in this century a man named Longworth decided to open the hole, and for several years he poured money into it. He hit water, which flooded the workings. He bought pumps, which proved inadequate. He teamed up with a San Antonio lawyer, Judge J. R. Norton.

Judge Norton, it turned out, had been chasing the same lode for years. He bought pumps and moved rocks by the ton, but the water seemed to be a permanent fixture. Eventually Longworth died and the Judge formed a new partnership. At this point, the most colorful figure since James Bowie himself enters the story.

Princess Wenonah, she called herself, when she was a high-class cooch dancer in stagey Indian costumes on the vaudeville boards. "The Comanche Princess! She dances with snakes!" She played with Pawnee Bill's Wild West Show, P. T. Barnum's circus, and as a single in New York and parts of Europe. Playbills from her show still exist.

Her real first name was Martha. She was the thirteenth child of a German who landed at Indianola in 1836 and an Indian woman who was supposed to be the daughter of a Comanche named Black Bear. Black Bear was alleged to be a chief, and he may have been—any Comanche who ever led more than one successful war party was quite legitimately a "war chief." The Princess was born in 1868 in San Antonio and was in her late sixties when she and Judge Norton teamed up, although she is said to have looked under fifty. She was, by her photographs, an extremely handsome woman, not delicately beautiful, but sturdily good-looking and imposing of figure.

According to Martha/Wenonah, she got her knowledge of the silver at Menard from Comanche legend handed down through her mother and grandfather, while Judge Norton's information came from ancient Spanish archives. Between them, they decided that the Calf Creek Fight had actually taken place on Silver Creek, and they located a grave that contained not merely human bones, but the remains of a rifle or musket and a knife. This, they said, was Tom McCaslin's burial site. It apparently never occurred to anyone to have the bones examined by a competent archaeologist. White people seldom buried the deceased's weapons with him. Indians almost invariably did. For some reason, the Princess and the Judge attached extreme importance to the exact location of McCaslin's bones.

Princess Wenonah and Judge Norton proceeded to sink over $80,000 (depression era) into the great hole at Silver Creek, of which some $20,000 was the remnant of the Princess's once considerable fortune. There are those who insinuate that the Princess was working a con on the old Judge, but con artists do not sink their own money, year after year, into a swindle. Princess Wenonah believed in whatever it was she thought they had. In any case, she and the Judge were very secretive about it. Only once did the Judge open up about it. He remarked that when they eventually did penetrate the treasure-chamber "it will cause a sensation second only to the opening of King Tut's tomb."

In 1943 the Comanche Princess died of cancer. She is buried near the mine. The Judge was killed in 1948 in the explosion of a gasoline stove in a cabin near the mine. Whatever she was, con artist or real, Princess Wenonah was one of a kind; she was the stuff of which legends are made.

Today the great hole Dixon, Fleming, Ezell, and Stroud began in the summer of 1866 is known as the "egg-shaped basin," and the reason for the name is apparent. It is a massive ovoid hole, perhaps a hundred feet long by fifty wide. At one time nearly seventy feet deep, it has been filled in to a depth of less than twenty feet, and a pecan tree as big around as a man's thigh grows in the fill. Around it are numerous concrete-tiled shafts, and over them the rusted remains of various types of mining equipment. An ancient tree trunk is preserved by a steel fence, and there is alleged to be an arrow carved on it, pointing down. Try as I might, I could not distinguish the arrow. It is supposed to point downward alongside a tiled shaft labeled SILVER MINE. At the bottom of the shaft there is only water.

The rumors about the shafts on Silver Creek fly thick and

fast. Bullion, treasure, silver ore—just what is there? Nobody knows for sure, but there is something. The copper pegs and the turkey-egg–sized flint and the *metate* marked EXCAVAD had been there a long time when the four San Marcans dug them out in 1866. Somebody put them there, and since they were put there when Menard County was Comanchería, they were not put out for health reasons. There was a reason, and it can be found at the bottom of the long and twisting tunnel of the Las Iguanas Mine. The only part of the legend that doesn't fit is Jim Bowie.

CHAPTER XI

The Mining Companies of the Llano

There are any number of ways to annoy a resident of the Red Hills enough to get yourself shot, but you really have to work at most of them, for these descendents of Texas pioneers are of remarkably even temperament. You can go so far as to steal a sheep or a goat—though not a beef—and if you're hungry and have a house full of hungry kids you are more likely to get offers of help than a jail sentence.

If, however, you announce that you are forming a joint stock company to open a mining venture in the granite, things change rapidly. Brows furrow in outrage, and from behind pickup seats, out of closets, and from the depths of bureau drawers emerges an assortment of cartridge-loading ordnance that would scare a Central American *caudillo* into nightmares. The one who commits this social error will be lucky to escape wearing a Tupelo Tuxedo and riding a pinewood racehorse—tar, feathers, and a rail. The people of the Red Hills do not think highly of stock company mining ventures. There is a reason for it.

Some years ago in Dallas I met a man who, as the expression goes, "is kin" in the Red Hills, Mason County to be specific. He'd gone to college at SMU and grown up to be, of all things, a stockbroker. We fell to talking about the hills, about silver, and about stock companies.

"You know," he said, "if you wanted to know about all the stock companies that issued mining stock and papered Llano and Mason and Burnet counties with junk, you should have asked me about two years ago. My granddaddy was an all-day sucker with a milk chocolate center when it came to mining stock, either gold or silver, and I reckon he bought stock in might near every company that ever issued mining stock in the area. He had a big strongbox just jam full of some of the prettiest three-color-printed, gilt-edged stock certificates I ever saw. When he wasn't around, my grandma used to let me play with 'em—used 'em for play money. When Grandpa died my dad went through the whole mess and there wasn't a one of 'em worth the paper it was printed on. He was gonna burn 'em, but then he got a better idea. The old outhouse had lots of cracks and leaks in it, and most of those certificates were printed on real high quality paper. Daddy got some wallpaper paste and papered the inside of the privy with 'em. I remember when I was a little kid, sitting in the privy and reading the stock certificates on the walls. Pity, though—a couple of my kid cousins were playing cowboy and Indians in the old privy a couple of years ago. The house has had indoor plumbing since the forties and the old thing didn't stink any more. Anyway, it was around either Thanksgiving or Christmas and we were all down at the old home place for the holidays, and it was cold so the kids decided to build a campfire inside the old thing and damned if they didn't burn it down."

I asked if he could remember the names of the companies.

"Just one. I reckon most of those companies incorporated with a job printer and the corporate assets were a couple of fast saddlehorses for the promoters to skip town on. One of them—I remember it because it was just about at eye level and besides it was the fanciest certificate of all, all engraving and colors and Old English print—was the Llano and Great Western Mining and Smelting Corporation. I'll bet I read that one a hundred times. It was a hundred-share certificate, and Grandpa had paid $300 for it in 1899. I remember one line on it in particular: 'A joint stock company incorporated under the laws of Delaware. Offices: Llano, Texas, and Dover, Delaware.' I remember wondering what Delaware had to do with a silver mine in Llano County."

Since I, too, had a "stock nut" in the family—my great-grandfather, another all-day sucker with a milk chocolate center, whose specialty was oil stocks hawked door-to-door in New Orleans during the 1920's—I could sympathize. I still have some stock certificates that read "Incorporated under the laws of Delaware" (long a haven for stock-company promotions of doubtful legitimacy), and I, too, used them for play money when

I was a kid. Unfortunately the ones my great-granddaddy bought were printed on thin paper that is too light to use for insulating a privy and too slick for any other practical purpose. I still take them out and look at them occasionally to remind myself that the $300 that each one represents would have bought, in 1920, fifteen ounces of gold bullion and that it would take almost $9,000 to buy that same amount of gold today.

Stock companies, as you may have gathered, have a poor reputation in rural Texas. Stock swindles by the hundreds—land, oil, gold and silver, salt, uranium, what-have-you—have victimized rural Texans for generations. O. Henry's "Gentle Grafters," Jeff Peters, Andy Tucker, Buckingham Skinner, Parleyvoo Pickens, et al., were not creatures of pure imagination. Porter lived in Austin and New York during much of the great stock-swindle era of the late nineteenth century, and he drew from life.

Because of this, there is still deep distrust of the idea of "buying stock" among rural Texans. During one of the recessions of the early 1960's I got interested in the stock market, and noted that the stock in Walt Disney Productions had dropped to a fantastic low. I had some money in an account that my dad had to co-sign, and I went to him with the idea of investing the entire $600 or so in Disney and making a substantial profit when the stock market went back up. Dad's reply has probably killed more youthful money-making schemes than any other, because it is typically rural Texas: "Boy, any time you want to put money in stock, put it in livestock. When the bottom falls out you can eat a cow. You'll play hell eatin' a piece of paper."

As far back as the 1850's, on the heels of the great California gold rush, a series of newspaper articles succeeded in starting a sort of minature gold rush to the Texas hills. Now, there is gold in the Red Hills, mostly placer gold, and most of it is both difficult and expensive to recover from surface deposits; but the strong suit of the Llano country has always been silver, not gold. Besides, the Comanches and Apaches who disputed all land titles in the area were far less tractable than the long-subjugated mission Indians of California. Still, several companies set up headquarters in San Antonio and Austin hotel rooms and papered the area with stock certificates before the promoters left by the dark of the moon for unannounced destinations.

In 1861 Texas seceded from the Union and, against the advice and wishes of the governor and senior statesman of Texas politics, Sam Houston, joined the Confederacy. Houston's name may have been an anathema to the fire-eating secessionists like Louis T. Wigfall, the Texas senator who supposedly "turned the US Senate into a forum where only an expert pistol shot could speak freely," but it remained a respected one in the Red Hills, where many of the veterans of the revolution settled. Nearly every Red Hills hamlet boasted one or more grizzled old-timers who had "fit with old Sam in '36," and one in particular, Sion Reckord Bostick, one of the five young Texans who captured Santa Anna after San Jacinto, was a potent force in local politics in and around San Saba.

In addition, the Red Hills were home to the Texas Germans, mostly liberal intellectuals who had fled Metternich's reordering of Europe in the 1840's. They were, as a group, staunchly pro-Union, and, although their descendants fly the Stars and Bars on occasion today, staunchly abolitionist. The German enclaves at Fredericksburg, San Antonio, New Braunfels/San Marcos, and Seguin produced three regiments—the 1st and 2nd Texas Cavalry and the 1st Texas Infantry—for the Union.

The Confederacy, however, had Texas, and with it, the minerals of the Red Hills. As everyone knows, the Confederacy ran a printing press rather than a treasury, but some gold and silver was produced for overseas trade. We know, both from history and from romantic Southern novels, most notably *Gone with the Wind*, that a lot of the Confederate bullion came from the melting down of silver and gold heirlooms and even the wedding bands of Southern women, but some of it apparently came from mining. The granite uplifts of the southern Appalachians, most notably the area around Stone Mountain, Georgia, northeast of Atlanta, had produced limited quantities of gold in the past. The old, mostly unproductive mines were reopened and, using slave labor, some gold was mined there.

We should not assume that no attempts were made to mine the Red Hills, but the area north of San Antonio and west of the Colorado was a hostile environment in more ways than one. The Nickajack country of north Georgia was somewhat Union in sentiment, but most of that sentiment evaporated in the first years of the war. The strongly pro-Union, or at least antisecessionist, sentiment of the Red Hills lasted for the duration and later surfaced in a bloody series of feuds known as the Mason County War. Not only were the whites unfriendly, but the Indians, emboldened by the absence of troops, either Federal or Confederate, from the frontier forts, became a major problem.

Gold mining took place, with some small success, in the sandhills south of Seguin—an area inhabited by non-German whites known to the area Germans by the uncomplimentary term "raggedys"—and around Gonzales. No one yet, however, has turned up any documentation of Confederate attempts to mine gold and silver in the Llano area. The Confederacy did mine a much more immediate necessity not too far from Llano, though. The cave known today as Longhorn Cavern contained a vast deposit of bat guano, which is rich in potassium nitrate, saltpeter, an essential ingredient in gunpowder. While the rest of the South urged its delicate ladies to save the contents of their chamber pots for the manufacture of "nitre," and gleeful journalists published indelicate poetry about the practice, Texas women were spared this humiliation by the existence of several generations' supply, courtesy of the bats of Longhorn Cavern.

When the war ended, Texas, unlike most of the South, was spared the excesses of Reconstruction for almost five years. It was not until the election of Edmund J. Davis, a Radical Republican from Corpus Christi, in 1870, that the full force of political "Reconstruction" fell on the state. Ironically, it was during this period that the earliest true efforts to organize mining companies to work the Llano minerals began. The earliest of these, the Sam Houston Mining, Smelting, and Rare Minerals Company, was born about 1871. No charter exists in either the state archives or the office of the secretary of state for this company, and its existence is known only from a few bills for supplies and foodstuffs. The fact that these bills exist indicates that it operated for a time, but where, when, and what it accomplished remains a mystery.

That same year the state legislature chartered a limited stock company called the Llano Mining Company. The organizers were W. J. Locke, Fritz Tegener, G. H. Kalteyer, B. F. Casey, William Lockhart, E. D. Hall, P. G. Temple, "and their associates." It was capitalized at an ambitious $500,000, but the 1870's were a time of great inflation. The company was granted the right to acquire real estate for "the mining of gold, silver, copper, and lead, or any other minerals," and to own buildings and means of transportation for moving ore and operating a mine, and to smelt ore. One section of the legislative charter empowered the company to use timber or other material found on public land adjacent to its mine or mines for constructing buildings or otherwise operating the mines. This company issued 5,000 $100 shares, and there is no mention in the charter of how the capital was raised or who held which shares. No corporate history exists, and we don't know what, if anything, the company actually did. The presence of the two German names in the charter is significant. Texas Germans, especially those around Fredericksburg, were largely Republican. Their names and support were probably necessary to get the document through the legislature.

In 1874 Richard Coke was elected governor and Davis left office under heavy guard to prevent his being assassinated. He was escorted out of the state, and Texas rewrote its constitution to ensure that no future governor would ever wield as much power as Davis had. One of the benefits, at least for historians, of the 1876 constitution was the revision of the method of chartering corporations. No longer did the legislature issue charters; instead companies were required to submit copies of their charters to the office of the secretary of state. The charters had to contain, among other things, the names and home addresses of the principals, the amount of stock to be issued and to whom, the term of years for which the corporation was to exist, and a great many other details that were no doubt tedious to the founders of the company but provide a wealth of detail for people who pore over musty papers.

In 1876, the year of the new constitution, A.W. DeBerry, secretary of state, received the handwritten charter of the San Saba Mining Company, headquartered in Austin. The organizers were C. R. Johns, W. von Rosenberg, F. Everett, J.W. Fleming, and Hugh H. Haynie. All but Everett were Austinites, Everett being a resident of San Saba. And all were shareholders in C. R. Johns and Company, which owned most of the San Saba Mining Company.

The company was formed to last fifty years, and to conduct a general mining business "on the waters of the San Saba, Llano, and Colorado Rivers, and at any other points within the limits of the State of Texas that to the Directors of said Corporation may seem proper." The company was capitalized at a very ambitious $600,000, of which $194,000 was appropriated for the development of the mines. The remaining $406,000 was to be "credited to the accounts of and owned by" C. R. Johns and Company ($174,000), Hugh H. Haynie ($174,000), and J.W. Fleming ($58,000), and their stock was declared forever nonassessable. C. R. Johns and Company was to be the principal supplier of leases, and Johns himself was president of both companies, while Everett was secretary and treasurer of the mining company. Only the charter is on file, no further business having been filed with the secretary of state's office. The company apparently accomplished nothing of note and faded into obscurity.

In 1902 a group of Hill Country folks decided to start their own shoestring mining company, appropriately named the Gopher Hole Mining Company. The Gopher Hole was truly a poor man's mining company: the capital stock was $1,000, divided into twenty $50 shares. The organizers were R.T. Cooper of Williamson County and G. M. Watkins, A. L. Stubbs, L. C. Smith, and Samuel Spears of Llano County. The company was organized for fifty years to conduct a general mining business in Llano and adjoining counties and for the purpose of "purchasing and selling such property, products, by-products, goods, wares, and merchandise, and mining lands and mineral rights, and the making and sinking of shafts and excavations therein, and the purchase and erection of such machinery, plants, appliances, apparatus, and materials as may be reasonably necessary to the successful prosecution of such business." The Gopher Hole Mining Company, headquartered in Llano, began with lofty ambitions and apparently went nowhere. No corporate history is appended to the charter, and in 1950 the 51st Legislature declared the charter forfeit through inactivity, though its original life had two years to run.

In the spring of 1907, Dr. Herbert C. Bolton, the man who was to become known as the greatest authority on the Spanish period of Texas, took a typescript copy of Miranda's report, climbed on a horse, and with the journal in hand followed Miranda's tracks, landmark by landmark, from old San Fernando—now La Villita in downtown San Antonio—to Riley Mountain and the shaft known locally as the Boyd Shaft, which he identified positively as Miranda's Cueva de San José del Alcazar, the Lost San Saba Mine. You could do that sort of thing in the days when the hills around Bulverde weren't full of high-priced developments. Such was the reputation of the man that two years later, in 1909, a half-dozen or so wealthy men from the Llano area sat down at a table in a lawyer's office in that city and on a lined tablet wrote out in pencil the charter of the Los Almagres Mining Company.

The initial shareholders were W. H. Gaston of Dallas, who subscribed $500—Gaston Avenue in Dallas is named for his family—J. Farley of Dallas, $1,500; F. M. Ramsey of Lampasas, $2,000; Fernando Miller of Lampasas, $500; Dr. Bolton, who was then residing in Mexico City doing research, $500; F. T. Ramsey of Austin, $500; and C. C. Berry of San Saba, $1,000. The assets of the company were sundry cash and leases of 1,276 acres of land from R. and B. F. Boyd, 260 acres from J. A. Coursey and wife, 140 acres from W. R. Roberts and wife, and 197½ acres from C. C. Roberts. All of this land was in the immediate vicinity of Riley Mountain and along Honey Creek. The leases covered mineral rights in, on, and under the land. This original charter was dated March 31, 1909, and the funding and land transfer was recorded by Milton Harris, a notary public of Travis County, on April 7. The Los Almagres Mining Company was on its way.

The company set to work, digging a new hole alongside the original Spanish shaft and just incidentally dumping its spoil down the original hole, thereby enraging historians and archaeologists who would have liked to explore the original dig. Apparently the money ran low because on June 15, 1910, the corporation took in eleven new shareholders, nine from Dallas and two more Farleys from Austin. The new shareholders subscribed $3,500 in additional capital and actually paid in $1,750 cash, raising the capital stock of the company to $6,500. On the same day the stock was expanded to $10,000 and sworn before

John C. Oatman, attorney and notary public in Llano.

By February 23, 1911, the corporation was interested in more stock. On that day J. Farley, F. M. Ramsey, and Fernando Miller, company officers, appeared before Wilburn Oatman, lawyer and notary and John C. Oatman's brother, and increased the capital stock to $50,000. Of this, $40,000 was bought by Farley, who paid by "purchase and present ownership of the minerals which have been discovered and developed and are worth twice the value of the increased capital stock and more and mineral rights on about 1676 acres of land in Llano County, Texas. . . ." In addition, Ramsey purchased the mineral rights to 400 acres of land from W. R. Roberts and his wife, and some $4,000 cash was paid to the secretary-treasurer of the company by Farley. It is interesting to note that the phrase "which have been discovered and developed and are worth twice the value of the increased capital stock and more" was added in pen to the original typewritten affidavit and there is no way to determine when it was added or by whom.

On May 7, 1912, a stockholders' meeting was held and the majority of the stockholders—which may well have been one man, J. Farley, who held better than 80 percent of the stock—voted to change the place of business from Llano to Dallas, Farley's hometown. The board of directors changed the location and certified the change to the secretary of state, as required by law, on April 3, 1913.

At this point the corporate history, as recorded in the secretary of state's office, ends. The company, which had actually mined the area, collapsed with the rest of the country in 1929, and so far as we know it was the last stock company organized to work the original San Saba Mine. The land around the shaft belongs currently to A.W. and Will Moursund, a father-and-son firm of attorneys, in Round Mountain, Texas. The Moursunds have, through long and painstaking effort, traced down and acquired all the mineral rights. They are not saying whether or not they intend to mine silver at Cerro del Almagre.

Not all of the mining companies that sought silver and gold, and other minerals, in the central Texas area concentrated on the Red Hills of the Llano country. One, the San Saba Mining Corporation of San Antonio, chartered on November 22, 1934, aimed at the elusive Las Iguanas deposits around Menard. As indicated in the Obregón report, Las Iguanas was merely one of several silver deposits in what is now Menard County. The hole opened after the discovery of the *metate* marked EXCAVAD, which is probably the original entrance to Las Iguanas, was reopened in 1866 and has been worked steadily since the 1890's.

The organizers and directors of the company were J. Douglas McGuire, A. J. Lenzen, A. Betts, T. C. McGuire, and E. B. Craig, all of San Antonio, and the capital stock was "$10,000 — a tremendous sum in the 1930's — divided into 200 shares valued at $50 each. That's the last simple statement that can be made about the San Saba Mining Corporation.

According to an affidavit sworn before Gladys Brubaker, a notary public of Bexar County, the assets of the company consisted of "$10,000 in personal property, leases, equipment, materials, services, labor, and cash advanced and expended for the benefit of said corporation, all to the aggregate actual value of $10,904.50." Thereafter follows some three pages of itemized assets.

One of the primary, and remarkably inexpensive for the amount of paper devoted to it, assets is a mineral lease of 588.7 acres from W. D. Hale and his wife, Bessie Hale. The company paid the munificent sum of $1.00 for the lease. It is apparent that the company expected this lease to be questioned, for appended to the charter is an affidavit from Selma Walston, a notary in Menard, declaring that W. D. and his wife, Bessie, had appeared before her and sworn that they had in fact leased their land to the San Saba Mining Corporation for the sum of one dollar, and that "the said Bessie Hale, wife of W. D. Hale, having been examined by me privily and apart from her husband, and having the same fully explained to her, she, the said Bessie Hale, acknowledged such instrument to be her act and deed, and declared that she had willingly signed the same for the purposes and consideration therein expressed, and that she did not wish to retract it."

The original Hale lease is appended, and it is a remarkable document. For one dollar the San Saba Mining Corporation purchased the right, in effect, to totally destroy 588.7 acres of Menard County in a search for minable minerals (excluding petroleum or natural gas), with a steam shovel if necessary, in what may be the first strip mining lease in this part of the state. There is no obligation on the part of the corporation to restore the property once the stripping is completed. For the destruction of their land the Hales were to receive 10 percent of any recovery—less than most petroleum leases of the time, which generally assured the owner of the land or mineral rights one-eighth, or 12.5 percent of the recovery. Earlier and later leases vested owners in one-sixteenth of the recovery. Today's leases may go as high as one-fourth of the recovery.

A later affidavit contains what may be either an error or a change of heart. It lists the sum paid to the Hales as "ten dollars ($10.00)" rather than a single dollar.

The "services and labor" also contained some questionable items. A. J. Lenzen, who held himself out as a geologist, charged $350 to the company for a geological survey, examination, and analysis of prospective leases in and around Menard County, during a period of seven days. A sum of $50 a day in 1934 was princely, to say the least. T. C. McGuire received only $200 for himself and three assistants for the geographical survey of the Hale lease, and an eight-day trip for the entire group of organizers/directors from San Antonio to Kerrville, Junction, Menard, Brownwood, Brady, Llano, San Saba, Mason, and Fredericksburg—quite a distance, even on modern roads, and not an easy journey—cost, including travel expenses, transportation, board, and lodging for five men, only $150.

The rest of the assets consisted of a long list of equipment that might or might not have been useful in mining, ranging from $600 worth of camp equipment to an air compressor and two air hammers valued at $2,380, a "double drum Ersted Universal Hoist, three-speed model with material elevator spool equipment"—sounds impressive, whatever it is—valued at $1,800; a boom and gin pole valued at $100; and 1,000 bolts at 8¢ each. The last item on the list was a 1929 Nash six-passenger automobile valued at $500.

This Nash caused me to question the whole list, but finding someone who had been actively involved in the automobile business in 1934 is a little hard some fifty years after the fact. I finally found an ex-Canadian who had been buying and selling used cars around Detroit, Michigan, in the late 1920's and early 1930's. According to him, the value of the Nash, considering that it was five years old and had normal wear (which at that time would have been around 30,000 miles) and was in average or slightly better than average condition, not full of dents and no ripped upholstery, would have been about $125. Specifically, he said that if you got more than $125 for the thing you had a mask and a gun, assuming—and this, I hasten to add, is his statement, not mine—you could find a sucker damnfool enough to buy a Nash in the first place.

Detroit is a long way from San Antonio, but research into the back issues of San Antonio newspapers of the period indicates that you certainly could buy a Nash in San Antonio in 1934 for $500—several of them all at once, and have money left over. In fact, you could come very close to buying a brand-new Ford V-8 coupe with a radio, a hot-air heater, and wire wheels, for that same $500.

I must not have been the first skeptic to look with uplifted eyebrows on the evaluation of the Nash, for appended to the assets sheet is an affidavit. It is signed by R. E. Steppenbeck, O. J. Watson, and R. T. Harrick, all of whom swear that they have five or more years' experience apiece in the purchase, sale, and trade of used automobiles of all makes and conditions, and they agree that they, together and separately, have appraised and evaluated a 1929 Nash six-passenger sedan, engine number A-52189, license number 67-174, at $500, and that "the same is a reasonable value and appraisal as based on the market value of an automobile in similar condition and the same make as of the present date." The affidavit concludes by stating that none of the three appraisers own any interest in the mining company and that none have received any remuneration beyond a normal appraisal for their services.

In fact, it seems apparent that every transaction and evaluation covered by the charter was expected to come under question, for every time somebody mentions a dollar in the charter there is an affidavit to back it up. Lenzen presents an affidavit for his services as a geologist, McGuire for his as a surveyor, everybody for the prospecting junket, and three more independent appraisers attest to the value of the assorted junk. The final affidavit is the one that changes the amount paid to the Hales for the lease from a singleton to a sawbuck.

There is one more item of note. The name of the company is the San Saba Mining Corporation, but all through the charter, the affidavits, and the leases the word "Corporation" is written in by hand over an erasure. This seems to indicate that for some reason the name had to be changed at the last minute, probably from Company. The 1876 San Saba Mining Company might well have been the conflict.

Today, other than extensive quarrying operations for Texas pink granite, the stone that makes the Red Hills red, and marble, there is but one mine in the area. In western Burnet County a graphite pit produces commercial graphite for such uses as lubricants and pencil leads.

CHAPTER XII
Is Anything Left?

On a chilly, damp Thursday evening in November 1979, as I was preparing to close my business for the night, a man I'd never seen before came in. When he introduced himself I recognized his name. I've known him by reputation for many years as a treasure hunter who has enjoyed considerable success.

"I hear you're huntin' that old San Saba mine," he said.

"Not just hunting," I said. "I think I've found it."

"On Honey Creek off the Llano—east Honey Creek, the one that runs out of the box canyon?"

"That's the right area," I said.

"Lotsa holes around there. Which one you figger is the right one?"

"It's up on the side of the mountain. Riley—that's Cerro del Almagre. It looks out toward the road. If it weren't for the trees, you could see it from 71."

"That's it, all right," he said. "Big old pile of pink dirt right in front of it. Me, I figger that hole's worked out—anyway, they sure didn't take anything out of it back in 1910 or whenever it was that they dug and left that big old winch up there. You figger the Spaniards got that?"

"A lot of it," I said. "Perry got the rest, I reckon."

"Ole Perry's a fair guess for it, I reckon," he said, "but I know a feller'll give you a fight over it. Claims he's got Perry's main hole spotted, smelter and all, up on the Little Llano. Anyway that hole's empty as a cowboy's back pocket. You reckon there's any silver left?"

"Probably not there—at least not in that particular hole. In the hills, yes."

"You're right," he said, and handed me what appeared to be a small, waterworn rock about the size but not the shape of a package of regular cigarettes. It was unusually heavy for its size and felt metallic. I rubbed at it with a towel, but the patina was too thick to be brushed away.

"Look at the bottom of it," he suggested.

I turned the rock over. Someone had taken a slice at it, apparently with a very tough, very sharp knife—a knife like the folding Buck Hunter he wore in a snap sheath at his belt. Inside the slice the "rock" was silvery white.

"*Plata blanca y pura,*" he said. "Assay runs between 90 and 97 percent."

"Texas?" I asked.

"Yep."

I turned the rock over in my hands. "You didn't pick this up around that old smelter on Packsaddle," I said. "This is water smooth."

"That's right," he said.

"This came out of a creek bottom," I said. "Either it was in a strip of black gravel or it wasn't too far from one. And it wasn't alone."

"You know your stuff," he said. "They aren't common as flint, but if a man knows where to look and don't mind gettin' some dirt under his fingernails, he can pick up four–five of those a day."

I tried to judge his reaction to my next remark. "Feller was to decide to start looking, Brady might be a good place to start."

He chuckled. "You wouldn't tire a good horse in the distance you're off," he said.

"Which creek?" I asked.

He took the silver nodule from my hand and pocketed it. "Hell, I ain't gonna take all the fun out of it. Find it yourself. I did—and I didn't get shot at doin' it."

The Red Hills of Texas are a granitic uplift, formed by the slow cooling and solidification of liquid rock many millions of years ago. The area is what is known as a batholith or deeply submerged rock, a mass measuring many miles in horizontal dimension and extending to unknown depths. The area, known specifically as the Red Hills or the Granite Hills or the Red Rock country or by a half-dozen other names, which encompasses Burnet, Llano, Mason, and parts of several other counties, is merely the exposed portion of the batholith. Red granite underlies much of the innocent-looking white limestone that surrounds the exposed portion.

Granitic uplifts like the one called the Llano Uplift, which is the proper geological name for the Red Hills, are the primary source of mineral wealth—gold, silver, lead, iron, copper, and precious stones—in the world. The Llano Uplift is one of the world's oldest known exposed uplifts—far older, for example, than the one that forms most of the Rockies. A look at any map of metallic mineral production will show that the major producing areas are within or adjacent to granitic uplifts. In the United States, precious metals have been found and mined extensively in North Georgia, the Black Hills of the Dakotas, all along the Rocky Mountain chain, all along the Sierra Nevadas, and in the Alaska Range, all of which contain granitic uplifts. It would stand to reason, then, that a similar uplift in central Texas should produce similar mineral wealth. So far it hasn't, so far as we know, but is that because there isn't any, or is it because nobody has ever really bothered to make a serious hunt for it?

History has not favored the mineral exploitation of the Red Hills. From the time Don Manuel de Aldaco torpedoed Bernardo de Miranda's silver strike in the 1750's until the removal of price controls on precious metals in the United States in the 1970's, there were only about fifty years in which it was possible to exploit the Red Hills, and that one real chance was missed because it happened to coincide with major, proven mineral activity and other profitable economic activities elsewhere. Miranda's was the last chance for over a century for white men to make any major discoveries in the Llano country, and the Spaniards lost that one.

Because our high school and college history survey courses concentrate on the halls of Congress and where the bluecoat soldiers rode, we are woefully ignorant of many of the factors that influenced our history—not European factors, but American ones. Particularly we ignore what was going on in the great central heart of our country during the sixteenth, seventeenth, and eighteenth centuries.

Far to the north of Texas, in the hills of the Dakotas, western Minnesota, eastern Montana, and southern Canada, there lived a powerful, once nomadic Amerind nation. They called themselves *Lakotah*—the People. We call them Sioux. The Lakotahs had "progressed," in the white man's view, from being foot-slogging nomads to being settled farmers—the first step on the white man's twisting road to "civilization." Yet the Lakotahs had been, and remained, mighty and feared warriors, and where Lakotah lodges stood no tribe hunted—not even the powerful Shoshone nations, which included a group who called themselves *Ne-men-ni*—also, the People. We call them by the Ute word meaning "always my enemy," *Ko-man-seh*— Comanche.

In the mid-seventeenth century the Lakotahs acquired horses, the dogs of the Gods. In a matter of a very few years all the long centuries of "progress" were reversed and what was destined to become the most powerful Amerind nation there ever was burst onto the plains ahorse, hunting, and at war. Everybody else, including the Comanches, got out of the way.

The explosion of the Sioux onto the central plains of North America, together with their kinsmen and allies, the Cheyennes, affected the history of every tribe and state-to-be between the Mississippi and the Rockies. The Shoshones split, part moving away from the plains and into the mountains of western Colorado and Wyoming. Others, including some of the ones we later came to know as the Comanches, moved south. As the Sioux and Cheyennes continued to expand, the Comanches moved further south. By the 1790's much of what had been central Comanche range—Kansas, Nebraska, and northern Oklahoma— was Sioux and Cheyenne country. The Comanches had been pushed south into Oklahoma and Texas, and they were not happy about it.

The Red Hills of Texas had long been disputed by the Brothers of the Wolf—the Tonkawas, whom some tribes called by the darker title "Eaters of Men"—from the east, and by the multiplicity of related Athabascan tribes we call by the collective term "Apache" from the west. Both tribes had horses, and the Tonkawas have been characterized by one chronicler as "the most perfect horseback warriors in the world." The statement was written before the full onslaught of the Comanches. The Apaches, being primarily a mountain and desert people, never fully learned the use of horses in warfare.

The Comanches swept down from the north, and they were masters of horseback war—the inventors of the dread "Comanche wheel," which was the deadliest mode of horseback attack ever contrived before the invention of the repeating firearm. They had, after all, the best of teachers, the Sioux, and they learned in a school where the penalty for failure was annihilation. The Comanches spread as far south as San Antonio by the 1770's, and by 1800 the Red Hills and most of west central Texas was solidly Comanchería. For the next seventy years or so, the only white men able to settle west of the Colorado and have a reasonable expectation of keeping their hair without having to fight for it every day were the Texas Germans who, in the 1840's, made the only treaty with the Comanches that lasted.

Eventually—by the 1870's—the Comanches were pushed back onto the high plains by the combined efforts of the US Army, the Texas Rangers, and every citizen with a Colt and Winchester, and the Red Hills lay wide open for the white men. Unfortunately, somebody forgot to tell the Apaches. From their strongholds high in the Davis and Guadalupe mountains they raided west across the plains and into their old hunting ground, the Red Hills. They sent their comparatively small war parties out—the Apaches, being a desert people, seldom traveled in large groups—and did damage and spread terror far out of proportion to their numbers. It remained unsafe to go hunting silver and gold in the Red Hills.

The last Indian fight in the Red Hills involved Apaches, and it took place on the east slope of Packsaddle Mountain in 1876. Historians used to the raids of the Comanches scarcely deign to call it a battle. There were less than a dozen Apaches and not too many more white men. Those same historians fail to take into account the fact that even Geronimo seldom had more than a hundred warriors, and it took the combined strength of the US and Mexican armies to bring him to bay.

At long last the Red Hills were open to mineral exploitation, and nobody really cared. In the 1870's and 1880's when a man said "silver" he meant Arizona or Nevada and when he said "gold" he meant California, Colorado, or the Black Hills. Men who searched for wealth went north and west, following minerals or cattle trails.

Then came 1901 and Spindletop. Overnight "minerals" meant only one thing to a Texan—oil. The oil booms that spread across Texas in the teens, twenties, and thirties of the present century overshadowed everything else. Those who might have searched for silver and gold went instead to Sour Lake, Kilgore, Ranger, or Borger.

In the 1930's President Franklin D. Roosevelt effectively killed personal searches for silver and gold in the United States when he pegged the price of gold at $35 per troy ounce and the price of silver at $1.25 per troy ounce and prohibited almost all private ownership of gold bullion. The effect was to depress, in particular, the silver market and the value of silver bullion. It was not until President Richard M. Nixon, in the 1970's, released the price of silver and gold to the free market and made it legal again for Americans to hold gold bullion that it once more became profitable to hunt for silver and gold. By that time, most people had forgotten the mineral promise of the Red Hills.

The Boyd Shaft, Miranda's Los Almagres Mine, still exists, high on the slope of Riley Mountain in southeastern Llano County, the legendary Cerro del Almagre. The land, together with the full mineral rights, today belongs to the Moursund family of Round Mountain, just south of the Llano County line in Blanco County, on US 281. Permission to enter the land and look at the hole that started this—the original "Lost San Saba Mine"—is not difficult to obtain providing you are willing to take your own risks and not hold the Moursunds responsible for any injuries you might sustain while climbing fences or mountainsides or from any unfriendly reptiles you might meet. If you do decide to go and see the mine, the big rattlesnake who lives right in the hole is called Elmer. Say hello to him for me.

It is not my place to give explicit directions to the hole, because that might lead to too many unauthorized self-guided tours of the Moursunds' land, and they would certainly not thank me for it. Suffice it to say that once you've crossed Sandy Creek going north, you're very close. You have to get out on open range to get there, and there is a mile or more of walking involved—not because you can't drive closer, because you could, but you could also rip the oil pan out of your car on a hidden rock or stump in the weeds. Up on the east slope of Riley Mountain, a good two-thirds of the way up—and that mountain is mountain-goat steep—there is a very old, very dim trail. You won't see it unless you've tracked a few deer through brush, but it's there, and following it can be a test of your trailing ability. It is the old silver trail—the Spaniards brought ore down that trail by the *morral*-ful, loaded on mules. It ends in a very thick clump of liveoak and chapote—Mexican persimmon—and deep within that clump of thorns and shadows there is a pile of bright pink dirt—*almagre*. Atop the pile are the remains of an old winch or windlass that dates from the Los

Almagres Mining Company workings.

Behind the pile there is a large double hole about six feet across and perhaps twelve or fifteen feet long. It is shaped roughly like a pair of eyeglasses. The south part of the hole is only about six feet deep. The north part is very deep, and if the light is right or you have a flashlight you can see several long cedar poles a long way down. The shallow shaft is the Spanish one; the deeper hole, the Los Almagres Mining Company stope. Originally the Spanish shaft was much deeper, but the diggers of the later hole dumped their spoil down it. You are looking at the oldest positive indication of white men in central Texas— the original Lost San Saba Mine. For more than two centuries, men have searched, fought, murdered, and died for what you see here.

Now, don't go taking this book and trying to use my directions to find the hole, because you can't do it and besides, if you are caught stomping around on private land without permission you won't see the Lost San Saba Mine, you'll see another Llano County landmark—the jail. Trespassing is taken seriously.

Besides, Riley Mountain is about six miles long and the east slope covers probably 5,000 acres, and unless you have specific directions—which I haven't given and won't give—you are in for a very hot, uncomfortable tramp through liveoak, cedar, prickly pear, and chapote. In addition, the Boyd Shaft is not the only hole up there, and a couple of them don't announce themselves until you fall in. And then there are the unpleasantries—rattlesnakes, copperheads, scorpions, centipedes.

Not too far north of the first watercourse I've named runs Miranda's Arroyo San Miguel—Honey Creek today, once called Almagres Creek. All along the banks of the creek you will find holes and tunnels, some of them extensive, dating back in some cases to the 1830's or earlier. Many people have mined along Honey Creek, and not all of them have told what they found. A great deal of money and thousands of man-hours have been expended in these tunnels, and to assume it was all fruitless would be foolish. Miners may be crazy, as the old-timers claimed they were, but it is a special kind of insanity. If miners don't find anything, they go dig somewhere else. Some of these tunnels are much too extensive for nothing to have come out of them.

A little south of Honey Creek on Texas 71 lies Sandy Creek. Even if the state of Texas had not posted a neat green sign with the name on it, you would have no trouble identifying Sandy Creek. It is a braided watercourse running through a wide bed of bright red sand.

You can, if you're willing to expend the time and money, pan gold out of Sandy Creek. If you worked steadily for a week or two, panning tons of sand and treating the residue with quicksilver, then boiling the quicksilver off in a retort, you might take out a hundred dollars' worth of gold at today's prices—considerably less than a troy ounce—but you'd spend almost that much for the mercury you'd need to recover it. Sandy Creek gold is flour gold, fine and powdery, finer even than the "dust" of the California gold fields, and recovering it is extremely tedious and expensive besides. But if your itch to pan gold is overwhelming, Sandy Creek is one place to do it.

Roughly east by north of the old Spanish shaft on the slope of Riley Mountain where the whole "silver in the hills" tradition was launched by five Spanish adventurers in August 1755 lies the western slope of Llano County's most famous, most tradition-enhanced landmark—Packsaddle Mountain. As mountains go, Packsaddle isn't all that much. It wouldn't make a good foothill for the Davis or Guadalupe mountains of west Texas, and they are merely foothills for the Rockies, which are in turn overshadowed in North America by the magnificence of the Sierras and the Cascades. Only among the Smokies, the Alleghenies, the Ozarks, or the central Texas hills would Packsaddle seriously be called a mountain.

The size of a stick of dynamite is all out of proportion to the noise it will make or the damage it will do. So it is with Pack-saddle. For my money there are more rocks, rills, little hills, caves, cliffs, cracks, and places to break your bones on Pack-saddle Mountain than there are on any comparable amount of square mileage anywhere else on earth with the possible excep-tion of New Mexico's *Malpaís*. What Packsaddle lacks in size, it makes up for in sheer ruggedness. There are probably as many places to fall off on Packsaddle Mountain as there are on any given mountain in the Rockies, the Sierras, the Andes, the Alps, or the Himalayas, and while you won't fall as far on Pack-saddle you'll be just as dead when you hit.

Somewhere on Packsaddle there is a vein of lead with a strong percentage of silver that almost exactly matches the description of the vein Rezin P Bowie claimed he chopped "pure silver" out of with his tomahawk. It is called in legend the "Lost Blanco Mine," although many insist it is the "Bowie Mine" so long associated with the "Lost San Saba" story. It would better be termed the Lost Larimore Mine or the Lost Rowland Mine or even the Lost RJR Mine.

Old Man Larimore—that's all legend tells us of his name—was one of the earliest permanent Anglo settlers in what is now Llano County, and by all accounts he was cut from hickory with the bark left on. He settled on Packsaddle and made it his hunting and ranching ground back in the 1840's when land was free for the taking if a man had the sand to go and take it. Larimore had the sand, and plenty to spare. He fought Indians, claim jumpers, land swindlers, the weather, wild animals, and the country itself to build a fair ranching operation. One after-noon while he was hunting javelinas, he chased three of them into a den somewhere on the slopes of Packsaddle. He settled down to smoke them out by building a fire in front of the opening to the den, feeding it green leaves so it would smoke heavily, and fanning the smoke into the hole. While he worked, he examined the outline of the den and realized that the entrance to this "cave" was far too regular to be natural—this was a hole someone had dug, and from all appearances the digging was not recent. Even then the legends of silver and gold in the hills were rampant, and he decided to investigate.

After the peccaries had been smoked out, shot, gutted, and hung, he took a torch and went into the hole. Inside he found a vein of almost pure metal, lead with a high percentage of silver. Larimore had no real need for silver, but he did need lead for bullets, and his mine furnished an inexhaustible supply. He worked the mine for twenty years or so, taking out fifty to a hundred pounds of metal at a time and making bullets from it, possibly using the silver produced (or at least part of it) to purchase such necessities as flour, salt, gunpowder, and tobacco. He was apparently also bothered by people who wanted to know where the silver came from.

Larimore didn't go around telling the world he had a silver mine, and for good reason. Besides claim jumpers, there was a fair chance the Republic or state of Texas would have taken his mine away from him. We Texans, having so long prided ourselves on the idea that our land is ours from the surface to Hell and in between, mostly don't recall that this has been true only since 1866. Before that the Republic and state of Texas owned all surface and subsurface minerals, following Spanish and Mexican law. It was in 1866, in the Sal del Rey decision regarding a deposit of surface salt near the King Ranch in south Texas, the landowner was vested with ownership of surface and subsurface minerals.

In 1860 Larimore decided he'd had enough. He was no longer young, and the constant fighting was more than he could take. He decided to leave the hills forever, and to conceal his mine so thoroughly that no man would ever find it again. To do so he enlisted the help of a younger neighbor, Robert James Rowland.

Larimore and Jim Rowland turned the course of a gully on

the side of Packsaddle Mountain, directing runoff from spring rain into the mouth of the hole and filling it with silt. Over the hole they placed a flat rock, shoveled dirt over the rock, and sowed it with grass seed.

Rowland was less than anxious, it would seem, that the mine be lost forever. He carved his initials—RJR—into the rock, and proceeded to make a "magic circle" of landmarks that would lead a knowledgeable person to the mine. The circle included, besides the rock marked RJR, another rock marked with two crosses, a large cedar tree with a dirk or dagger carved on it and a rosary "buried" in it, a somewhat smaller cedar tree with a pick and shovel and RJR carved on it, and a cave "guarded" by a rattlesnake. All these marks are within a "magic circle" supposed to be 100 yards in diameter.

Of all these landmarks, the chances are very good that only the two rocks, one marked with crosses and the other with RJR, survive to this day. Packsaddle has been cut over for cedar a number of times in the intervening years and it hardly seems likely that Jim Rowland's two cedars would have been spared the cedar-cutter's axe. The cave guarded by a rattlesnake may still be there, but unless the guardian snake is another of Rowland's carvings it has probably long since departed.

All this carving of pictures and initials on things seems to indicate that Jim Rowland was the sort of feller who liked to carve pictures on things. A rock with RJR cut into it has been found, but for the moment its location will remain a secret save to say that it is generally in the right area to be the right rock. At some future time, I hope not too far in the future, the finder has agreed to guide me to that rock. Whether it is *the* rock upon which Jim Rowland carved his initials in 1860 or merely *a* rock upon which Rowland or someone else carved RJR at another time remains to be seen.

Whether or not James and Rezin P Bowie, Tom McCaslin, Matt Doyal, and all the others, nine or fourteen or twenty-five or however many in number, actually found silver in the hills that wasn't tied to the back of the Mexican government's mules is a moot point. What is agreed, however, is that they did tangle with some Indians, and that there was a pretty fair scrap—maybe more than one—when they did. Menard, Mason, Llano, and McCulloch counties all have their own locations for the fight—pretty close to one per teller of the tale. At a lot of these locations there were quite obviously fights, and from the bullet pocks still visible on rocks and in ancient liveoaks, some of these fights approached epic proportions.

Folks seem to overlook the obvious. Jim Bowie ain't the only feller ever fit the Injuns in the Red Hills. Bowie, it is true, fought the Indians there, but so did a lot of other folks. Bowie probably fought Indians several times, but if he fought Indians everywhere folks claim he did, he sure never found any silver—he spent all his time fighting Indians. A lot of frontiersmen who probably ought to be legendary figures in their own right and a lot of battles that would probably make awfully good stories if they were told are going unrecognized, untold, and forgotten because of this tendency to attribute every ring of rocks and bullet-marked tree in a five- or six-county area to Jim Bowie and party. When I was twelve, back in the early 1950's, I burned a little powder in the Red Hills myself. On one of the Capps ranches in Mason County I amused msyelf by target-shooting at a large knot on a big liveoak. I pumped fifteen .22 long rifles out of an old Winchester into my impromptu target, and in the ensuing thirty-plus years the bark has probably grown around the bullet holes enough so that they look very old indeed. It would not surprise me greatly if someday someone attributes that site, too, to Jim Bowie.

Among the many disputed locations for the fight of November 1831—the Calf Creek Fight—are two in Menard County. One is in the bed of Silver Creek about a half mile above the hole called the "silver mine," and the other is where a rough ring of rocks and downed timber lay in a dry wash east of Menard once called Jackson's Creek. In a letter of dubious authorship attributed to Rezin P Bowie, there is a statement that the fight took place "six miles east of the old fort." Jackson's Creek is roughly six miles down the east-flowing San Saba from the old *presidio*, but this site has been largely ignored.

The state of Texas, in the flurry of historical interest that accompanied the centennial of independence in 1936, chose a site and put up a monument near the Calf Creek community in southwestern McCulloch County, east of the ranch road that runs through the now defunct town. The monument stood in a lonely pasture for years, but was eventually moved to the roadside so people could see it. The state's chosen site is roughly 200 yards east of the present location of the monument. Matt Doyal, son of Old Matt and father of Ralph Doyal, always claimed that the state was "pretty close, but not right on" the spot his father showed him, where he and Jim Bowie fought Indians in 1831.

One thing consistently ignored is water. One of the more persistent legends connected with the fight—and there are many more such legends than the time involved would have allowed—is the sending of Bowie's black servant, Charles, for water. As the story goes, the frontiersmen ran out of water during the battle. Breathing the stifling, sulphur-laden smoke of black gunpowder brings on a powerful thirst, and the frontiersmen were suffering. Below the breastwork but within running range and rifle cover there was a large spring. Bowie ordered his servant to get a bucket and fetch some water.

Understandably, the black man objected. There were, after all, Indians out there. They did not customarily scalp black men, but since Estevánico they had shown no reluctance whatever to killing black men. Bowie is supposed to have pulled his legendary knife, tested the keen edge with his thumb, and asked Charles if he feared Indians or Jim Bowie the most. The black man went for water twice, got it both times, and returned safely under the covering fire of the white men's rifles.

There is no spring within running and rifle range of the site where the state put up the monument. There is no spring above or below the "fort" at Jackson's Creek, and there is no spring at Silver Creek. Bowie's battlefield must have a spring.

On the west side of the highway that runs through Calf Creek, almost exactly opposite the monument, lies a small ranch owned by Clyde and Eddith Harlow. About three-quarters of a mile west of the monument, across a field and a small hill, and in a draw, there is a large permanent spring that has been known since white men settled permanently in McCulloch County in the 1840's as the best place to get water even in the driest times. Clyde Harlow has lived on his land since 1924, and he has never known the spring to go dry, not even in the great droughts of the 1930's and the 1950's. One of the reasons his father bought that particular piece of land, he says, is that the spring didn't go dry in the most severe drought of the twentieth century, the great dry of 1918.

Above the spring there is a large flat area covered with great slabs of limestone, some of which are set on edge. They could conceivably be remnants of a breastwork, and more important, it is close enough to the spring for a young and fleet-footed man to run back and forth for water.

It is alleged that Tom McCaslin died in the fight, but Matt Doyal did not mention that. "McCaslin's grave" has been as diligently sought as the battlefield itself. In a small draw at the edge of the field east of the spring there was for years an oblong area about six feet by three feet that was surrounded by rocks. It did not look accidental. Back in the 1960's Clyde Harlow decided to put in a dirt tank in the draw. He hired a bulldozer and the blade cut into the ring of rocks. It was a grave—human bones, unencumbered by a box, tumbled out. This was as arguably a white man's grave—no weapons or grave goods were interred—as the grave at Silver Creek was arguably an Indian's from the presence of a gun and knife. In addition, the ring of rocks is a white man's type of marker. The bones were reinterred at another spot, and the site of McCaslin's grave—if it was McCaslin's—is on the eastern edge of Clyde Harlow's new tank.

There is no way to prove, some 150 years after the fight, that Jim Bowie's 1831 battle was fought on Clyde Harlow's ranch, but Harlow has the necessary spring, and there is that unmarked grave that, unlike the unmarked grave at Silver Creek, is most likely a white man's. The only way to prove it would be to locate the three mule-loads of silver buried in the immediate vicinity of the breastwork. If that silver is found, the battlefield will be located once and for all. Without it, nobody knows for sure.

There was once a story about a Comanche named Yellow Wolf. Dobie told it, but he misplaced it. Yellow Wolf brought chunks of raw silver to be hammered into ornaments for his clothing, hair, and horse trappings to a blacksmith shop on the banks of the South San Gabriel just below the site of the present town of Liberty Hill. Up until the 1960's the foundations of the old shop were still visible, but development since then has obliterated them.

The descriptions of the chunks of silver the Comanche brought in are not detailed enough to tell whether they were mined, picked up out of the tailings of a slag pile, or were waterworn nodules like the one I examined in 1979. He was asked where he got it.

"Three suns west," Dobie says the Indian replied.

A Comanche could ride a long way between sunup and sundown—anywhere from fifty to a hundred miles, depending on how hard he pushed himself, whether or not he was being chased, and whether or not he cared if he killed his horse. To the northwest of Liberty Hill, 150 miles or thereabout, lies the geographical center of Texas. Not far from it you will find the town of Brady—and you wouldn't tire a good horse in the distance from Brady to where the chunk of silver I examined was picked up out of a creek bottom.

In the late 1860's, just after the War—that War, Yankee!—a couple of Burnet County boys sneaked out to go fishing. They were snatched from the creek bank by a dozen or so Indians—the account claims Comanches, but to most settlers all horseback Indians were Comanches until proved otherwise—and were taken, bound and blindfolded, on a long, fast, and wild ride deep into the Red Hills to the west. Directions and distances are uncertain, but the ride lasted from about midday until long after dark, and the boys noticed that during the ride the air turned cold and night birds began to call. The ride ended at a cave where the two boys were unbound and their blindfolds removed, but the entrance (and escape) was blocked by Indians.

The following day the boys noticed the Indians picking up pebbles from the floor of the cave, melting them in a small, cast-iron pot, and running bullets from the resulting metal. One of the boys slipped a dozen or so pebbles in his pocket.

Sometime during that afternoon one of the Indians showed up with a jug of busthead whiskey, and the entire party of Indians got cross-eyed drunk and passed out. The boys stepped over the Indians, got out, stole a horse—it had once been a white man's horse, accustomed to being mounted from the left, which probably saved some broken arms, since purely Indian horses were trained to be mounted from the right—and rode away into the night. Riding double all night and, with a few stops, all the next day, they arrived in Lampasas. The horse was identified as having been stolen from Lampasas. Given his head, he went home and took the boys with him.

The pebbles were assayed. They proved to be largely lead, but with a not inconsiderable amount of gold and silver in the metal, an unusual but apparently natural alloy. The cave is somewhere within about fifty miles of Burnet, probably to the west or northwest, and may be under the waters of Lake

Buchanan. As W. A. McDaniel, one of the boys, put it much later, "I went in darkness, I left in darkness, and the cave is still in darkness as far as I am concerned."

There are myriad stories in the Red Hills of digging Indian-fired musket balls out of the logs of the house after a sharp fight and finding that they had been molded of pure gold or pure silver. As we saw earlier, silver musket balls are unlikely—but then, Comanches and Indians in general were less particular about what they put in their guns than were white men. There's an old Kentucky tale about hearing the bullets from Indians' guns whine peculiarly and finding that the Indians were firing roundish creek-bottom rocks. Maybe they did shoot silver bullets, maybe even gold—who knows?

William Edward "Ed" Syers, Mr. OBT, who has made a career of digging out that which is unusual and obscure in Texas history and legend, several years ago encountered a rancher west of Llano who had an unusual feature on his ranch. The rancher was August Oestereich. When I tried to contact Mr. Oestereich in October 1980 I found that he had died and his ranch had been sold.

On the Oestereich ranch, as Ed Syers tells it, there was a most unusual hole. It looked a lot like the limestone sinks that are common further east, in the limestone country around Bertram, Liberty Hill, and Georgetown, but this one was in granite, and granite doesn't form sinks. According to Oestereich he went down the hole in 1947 and found that it had been dug out from underneath. At the bottom were horizontal timbered shafts, and in one of the shafts he found, amid the debris of collapse, human bones including at least one skull, old picks and other tools, and some badly weathered letters scratched on one wall. The words, he believed, were Spanish, but he could not read them.

Ed didn't go down the hole, and I was unable to contact the new absentee owners to get permission to go down myself. I've never seen the thing, but from the description it sounds very much like a ventilation shaft for a mine, and it would appear that someone was trapped inside when one of the tunnels collapsed. The entrance is lost or at least not recognized as a mine entrance. There are no dates, but the skeletons argue for some antiquity; a lack of local surrounding legend, for greater antiquity; and a timbered mineshaft, for a pretty extensive operation. The possible presence of Spanish-speaking miners argues for nothing in particular—over the years the primary source of cheap labor in the area has been Spanish-speaking people, so Spanish words on the wall don't necessarily mean Spanish-period mining. In fact, it would argue against it—the *mozos* who would have done the mining under the Spanish regime would most probably have been illiterate.

In the 1930's a WPA geology team dug test holes all over the Red Hills, and while most of the men were pretty close-mouthed about what their core borings brought up, some of them had a weakness for bottles of Pearl beer, and cold beer after a hot day loosens tongues. If you go into the Wagonwheel Cafe in Llano, just north of the square on Highway 16, and sample the chili (a little greasy, but not bad) and the conversation (salty, but informative) you'll find that some of those loose tongues talked about silver and gold, not traces, but in quantity, brought up by WPA borings. The WPA borings took place after President Roosevelt called in gold and forbade private citizens to hold bullion. It wasn't publicized for obvious reasons—a gold rush was the last thing the country needed at the time. It hasn't been publicized since, but the reason for that is less apparent.

In the early 1960's, purely out of curiosity, a group of students from the University of Texas at Austin decided to see if they could find gold in the Red Hills. Using pans, they worked a dozen or more creeks in the Llano-Burnet area. In two weeks, in the various creeks—and without really having any idea what they were doing—the five students washed out more than ten ounces of fine, powdery placer gold without once trespassing on private property without permission. The gold, which had a nominal value of $350, was sold for $200 to a man who had a permit to hold gold. The students didn't even make expenses. Today the gold would be worth thousands, and it can be sold almost at the corner drugstore for very nearly its market value.

In a section of the "Lost San Saba Mine" chapter of *Coronado's Children*, J. Frank Dobie attributed a tale he entitled "An Innocent Old Liar" to a well-known pioneer lawyer, D. Y. Portis. The tale was told to another lawyer, J. T. Estill, who apparently told it to Dobie. According to the story, back in 1876 Portis and several other men made up a party to go hunting for Jim Bowie's silver mine. Their guide was an old-timer who claimed to have been with Bowie everywhere but at the Alamo. He swore he had personally hacked pure silver out of Bowie's famous vein with his tomahawk.

The party searched for a week or more and then, as such parties often do, began to question whether or not they were chasing the proverbial, never-caught wild goose. They grabbed the old man, tossed a rope over a limb, and told him to tell a straight story or dance on air.

"There is no Bowie Mine," the old man is supposed to have said. "It is true that I was with Bowie, but the only thing we found was Indians. They turned us back, for we were only a handful. In after years, with Bowie and the others dead, I began telling about the mine. I told the story so often and so long that I came to believe it myself. I am a liar, but I have told you the truth."

According to Portis, not only was the old man not hanged, but in later years members of the party that threatened to hang him told his yarns as their own experiences. He concluded the tale by saying that when he had the right kind of audience he himself had never admitted failing to glimpse Jim Bowie's silver.

One can only wonder how many silver mine tales in the Red

Hills got started in the same way. I can truthfully state that I have looked upon the Lost San Saba Mine—two of them—for I have climbed the rough side of Riley Mountain, which is Miranda's Cerro del Almagre, and stared into the hole called the Boyd Shaft, which is Miranda's Cueva de San José del Alcazar, Los Almagres itself, and I have stood in the area known as the Egg-Shaped Basin three leagues west of the old Presidio San Saba and one league north of the river that is the entrance to the still-to-be-reopened Las Iguanas mine. As yet I have not looked on the vein of gleaming silver that is the ultimate goal of the seeker for the Lost San Saba Mine. I may never do so, but even if I don't, will I, when I am a crusty old-timer of seventy or so and considered "one of those old fools who wasted his time hunting that silver mine," when presented with a proper audience of credulous seekers after hidden silver and gold, be able to resist the ultimate temptation? Will I not also claim that I, Bowie knife in hand, crawled into a musty cave somewhere in the Red Hills of the Llano country and carved a chunk off Jim Bowie's vein of *plata pura?*

One of the earliest treasure hunts of which we have any record involves a Greek named Jason who rounded up a few pals, conned somebody into grubstaking the run—a pretty good grubstake, apparently, because it included an oar-and-sail ship large enough to carry the whole crew and provisions for what passed for an open-sea voyage three or four millennia before Christ—and set a course across the sea. He went in search of a legendary realm called Iberia where a breed of sheep was reputed to shed gold. For if you ignore Ray Harryhausen's fascinating movie and reread your Bulfinch, you'll find that the fleece itself was not reputed to be gold, but that "the women of that land are wont to comb their sheep daily, and from the fleece they extract flakes of gold."

But there really was a golden fleece, and it was almost, but not quite, as advertised. Ancient Iberian placer miners lined their gold-washing sluice trays with sheep hides, and when they washed the gold-bearing sands down the sluice, the gold particles were trapped in the wool. Every evening the Iberian women got the unpleasant chore of lifting the heavy, smelly, soaking sheep hides out of the sluices and running currycombs through the matted wool to extract the gold. They were still doing it in historic times.

Jason's disappointment, when he found out what he'd been chasing, must have been boundless. Since he couldn't sail home with a cargo of golden Brillo, he and his companions invented one hell of a yarn to take the homefolks' minds off the fact that they'd come home with empty pockets.

Treasure hunting is probably the world's third oldest vocation, right behind prostitution and armed robbery. Jason himself, the much-admired hero of Greek myth, was a pirate and an unsuccessful sheep thief to boot. It should not be remarkable, then, that the techniques used by thieves and those used by treasure hunters tended to overlap, with a little black magic thrown in for luck.

Even "necromancy," a catchall term for what is otherwise called "black magic," but specifically a form of wizardry dealing with the dead, has been associated with treasure hunting, most commonly through tokens associated with, and sometimes made from, dead people.

Probably the most common token of necromancy was the corpse candle, made from human fat, while a lesser known and more gruesome version is called a "Hand of Glory." The Hand of Glory was made, using suitable enchantments, from the right hand of an executed murderer. It was commonly dried, and could be used as a candlestick for holding a corpse candle, or, under certain circumstances, as a candle itself. The five fingers were set afire, and their light was supposed to reveal signs and symbols leading to buried or hidden treasure that had been magically concealed.

A number of years ago a self-described *brujo* or Mexican warlock gave me what he called a treasure candle. It was a flat blob of wax, artistically molded to resemble a human palm, with five wicks in the form of fingers sticking out at impossible angles. With it came explicit directions for use in finding treasure.

In the company of four companions you take your treasure candle to a place where you suspect buried or hidden treasure— the terms are not necessarily synonymous—may lie. You do this on a windy night, and promptly at midnight each member of the party grasps a finger-wick tightly. The leader lights each wick, repeating a long and involved incantation as he does so. Once the incantation is finished, the party must remain in absolute silence. The wick that remains lit longest in the wind points to the treasure. The party moves, repeats the lighting ceremony, and keeps going until a place is found where all five wicks continue to burn regardless of wind. There is no mention in the instructions about what you do if you burn all the wicks off before you find the right place.

Assuming you finally arrive at the right place, you are directly over the treasure you seek. The leader sprinkles the ground with holy water, repeats a second incantation as long, involved, and essentially nonsensical as the first, and the treasure may be dug up at leisure. If the holy water and the second incantation are omitted, the treasure is almost certain to vanish or to change magically into something worthless. Oh yes—if you find a place where all five wicks go out simultaneously, scram. The treasure is just beneath you, but it is guarded by malignant spirits and unsafe to remove.

My treasure candle and the copies I made of the incantations disappeared several moves ago, long before I got a chance to try it. I have seen, since, in a number of odd shops in places like San Antonio, Juárez, and Acuña, identical candles, but I've never quite had the nerve to offer to buy one. Besides, if you'll remember, you're not supposed to speak while hunting treasure with a treasure candle. The finger wicks on the ones I've seen are all of an inch and a quarter long, and how you'd "grasp one firmly" without burning the hell out of yourself I don't know. It's been my experience that people who suddenly burn themselves tend to mention the fact, usually in a loud voice, and that would spoil the charm.

The Hand of Glory is one of several dozen treasure finders we've inherited from past ages. Most of them don't work—and never have. I have, however, seen treasure, of a sort, found with another treasure-finding device that is at least as old as Egypt.

There is no scientific principle behind the age-old practice of dowsing. There is no way a forked stick of willow or peach wood or a pair of copper rods can find water or buried metal or anything else—but they do, with startling regularity. I speak from experience.

A good many years ago my father decided to sink a new water well on his Williamson County ranch. He knew he wanted it in the pasture about a half-mile east of the house, but he wasn't sure exactly where he wanted it, and in that hard limestone country a difference of fifty feet or so horizontally can mean a difference of several hundred feet of drilling at several dollars a foot. Now, my Dad is hardheaded, and he doesn't believe in much of anything besides God, but there was a water witcher in the country, and a number of hardheaded ranchers swore by the man's ability. Dad parted with twenty-five hard-come-by dollars and the dowser showed up.

He was a classic Texas water dowser, in his mid-sixties, tall, lean, and leathery, wearing a battered Stetson, a rusty black suit coat that had seen better days over an equally veteran white shirt, loose-fitting denim jeans with a hammerloop on the leg, and heavy brogan shoes. He drove a Ford pickup a year or two younger than Dad's, and in the gunrack in the rear window of the Ford there was, besides the expected lariat, walking-stick-cum-sheepcrook, and Winchester .30–30 carbine, a peeled, forked willow wand.

He took the Y-shaped stick in his hands to demonstrate his gift. In most illustrations of dowsing and in nearly all movies, the dowser is shown holding the switch parallel to the ground. According to this water witch, that is wrong. He held his hands at his sides, palms outward, and grasped the switch so that the end of it came about to his chin. When I held it, the fork came almost to eye level on me.

We went up in the pasture to where Dad wanted his new well, and the dowser went to work. I watched him closely, and when the wand dipped I could not see that he had done anything at all to make it do so. When it went down it did so suddenly, and by the sound the ends of the stick made scraping against the calluses on his hands, against some resistance.

"Mr. Eckhardt," he said, "you got water here—mighty good water, but deep. Seven, maybe eight hundred foot, maybe more. You'll hit a little seep before you get to the main water, but drill on past it. That seep'll run dry on you. The second water you hit, it's good. I was you, though, I'd be a mite careful in the drillin', 'cause there's somethin' mighty peculiar 'bout the way it pulls. Feels almost like there's somethin' between the surface and the water. I'm gonna see can I tell what it is."

He baited the switch with a succession of items: a dime, a gold ring, a copper wire, an iron bolt. It remained upright. At last he baited it with the oil bottle. The switch dipped slightly, the tip danced a little, and then it returned to the upright position. "Can't make it out," he admitted. "Seems like it's kinda kin to oil, sort of, but it sure ain't oil. If it was I'd a known it right then. She pulls strong to oil. Whatever it is, it's between you and the water, and I figure it'll pay to be careful when you drill."

It was almost ten years later and I was married and gone when Dad finally got around to drilling for water in the pasture. The drillers did hit the seep, just as the dowser said they would, and they also hit a pocket of natural gas under enough pressure to lift better than two hundred feet of heavy metal well-casing about five feet in the air. Natural gas is "kinda kin to oil, sort of." The water well is a good one and is, so far as I know, still pumping merrily away under an old Aermotor windmill.

Now, I don't know whether I believe in water witches or not. I know for a fact that there is water underlying the entire area there, the Trinity Sands stratum, and if you drill deep enough to hit it you'll always pull up water of some sort in west-central Williamson County. It may smell like bad eggs and go through you like a dose of castor oil, but it will be water, and it will make the grass grow and keep the cows alive. But what about the gas? Did he really find something with his Odessa crude-baited willow wand, or did he just make a lucky guess?

Anyone who has read *The Golden Bough* or almost any sword-and-sorcery novel will recognize "baiting the switch" as the Principle of Similarity, one of the basic principles of ritual magic. The idea is that things that look alike or are made of the same or similar substances tend to attract one another when brought in proximity. Tom Sawyer used it to find marbles, and it has been used in treasure hunting since time out of mind. It is scientifically invalid. Gold doesn't attract gold; oil doesn't attract oil. The witching stick or dowser's wand doesn't work either—it's scientifically impossible—but every now and then it goes ahead and works anyway, because willow sticks and the people who use them don't worry about what's scientifically impossible and what isn't.

My friend Mike Clemmer is about as far from a water witch as you can get. He's a Presbyterian elder and an adventuresome sort. He wouldn't touch ritual magic with somebody else's ten-foot pole. He works for Southwestern Bell, and as part of his job he finds buried electrical and telephone cables, water and gas mains, sewer pipes, and similar items before the ditching machine comes through.

Bell has perhaps the most advanced electronic laboratory in the world. You'd suppose, then, that Mike would carry something straight out of Buck Rogers—all sorts of dials and antennae and transistors and electronic whichits that don't even have names yet. Nope. He uses two two-foot pieces of copper wire.

I took Mike up on Brady Creek a while back, looking for some silver somebody is supposed to have buried on a ranch just west of Brady. Mike had his copper wires—they're known as dowsing rods, mineral rods, or Spanish rods. I had a fairly sophisticated electronic metal detector. Mike took his two L-shaped pieces of copper wire in his hands and started walking. In a moment the wires crossed. I ran my detector beneath them and it squealed. We dug up a 1940's vintage crown-top beer can, almost rusted away.

"It helps," Mike said, "to be fat. They work better for fat people than for skinny ones, and better for men than for women. Nobody knows why." He placed the short legs of the L's in my hands. "Hold them loose, so they can swing freely. Tuck your elbows into your sides, hold the tips about eight or ten inches apart, and start walking. If they're going to work for you, you'll know it the first time you walk over something metallic."

I took a couple of steps and the wires, without any help from me, crossed. "There's something directly under the cross," Mike said. "Now take another couple of steps and watch them try to cross behind you." I did, and the wires swung against my shoulders. We found a badly corroded rifle cartridge just below the surface.

You can, incidentally, if you're so minded and careless with your money, spend upwards of $100 for a pair of manufactured dowsing rods. They have all the modern conveniences—exotic alloy, swivel handles, little metal balls on the ends. You can also spend considerably less than a dollar for four feet of solid core copper wire, cut it in half, strip it, bend it, and it will work just as well. Oh yes—they don't work if you wear gloves while using them, and the colder it gets the less sensitive they are. When the temperature drops below freezing, they don't work at all.

Shortly after World War II a commercial metal detector, under the brand name M-Scope, came on the market. Though M-Scopes are still manufactured, they bear little if any resemblance to the early ones. The M-Scope was shaped like a mashed box kite, and you carried it the way Stan Laurel carried a ladder when he wanted to swat Oliver Hardy in the backside with it.

M-Scopes were expensive—more than $300 at a time when $20 would feed a family of four for a week—and not many of them were sold in the forties and fifties. Right after Korea, a lot of WW II surplus mine detectors came on the market for considerably less than the M-Scope, and they sold well. The owner/operators quickly found that the valuable finds they'd heard about in Europe were flukes. As a general rule, anything less than a cast-iron dutch oven that was deeper than a foot and a half and had buried more than six months wouldn't provoke a beep out of a mine detector. When they were taken down to the sands along the Texas coast to hunt for the fabulous treasures on Galveston and Padre islands the salt and mineral content of the sand either blanked them out or caused them to go wild.

A lot of people decided they could do better, and some of them really could. Detector electronics is a million dollar business today, and a good many of the biggest names in the industry got started on garage workbenches because that damned war surplus mine detector didn't work like cousin Ernie said it would. Not all the experimenters, however, knew what they were doing.

Doodlebugs and doodlebuggers—home-made treasure finders and their owner/operators—have been around a long time. Dobie mentioned what he called a "radio sleuth" being used near Menard in the 1920's, and the post-Korea boom in both prosperity and electronics technology led to metal detectors that worked, but these things and their users cannot be called doodlebugs and doodlebuggers. True doodlebuggers were a breed apart and were a dying breed even when I was in my teens. Still, there were a few of them around.

He was an old man when I knew him, and his device was housed in a home-made wooden box about twice as long and twice as deep, but no wider, than a man's shoe box. The wooden case didn't "mess up the works" but the handle, hinges, latch, and other appurtenances were metal. One side displayed a pushbutton wall switch, a Ford ammeter, and what appeared to be a radio dial. Inside I recognized a couple of 1½-volt dry cell doorbell batteries, what I now think was a radio rectifier, and something that looked suspiciously like what I found when, at age eight or so, I dismantled the black box that made Lionel Lines go round and round. There were a couple of radio vacuum tubes, lots of red, blue, green, black, and striped wires, and in one corner an open-ended Bakelite tube that was glued in place and didn't appear to be connected to anything.

He took out a glass cigar tube, poured a quantity of motor

oil in it from a can corked with a piece of red rag, and put the tube carefully into the bait hole. He pressed the white button on the switch, and while the machine warmed up he poured about half a teacup of motor oil into some sand nearby. He latched the box lid, picked the thing up by the screen door handle, and walked around the motor oil, holding the light socket out to the stain the way you might hold out a dog biscuit to an unfamiliar dog with large teeth. In a moment he let it slip from his fingers until it swung freely from the cord in his hand. He glanced at the ammeter, grunted, balanced the box on his knee while he twisted the dial, looked again at the ammeter and the socket. Then he turned to me.

"See how 'at bug's a-swingin'?" he asked. "Pickin' up 'at oil I put down. She's ready t' go."

Of course the socket was swinging. The way he was waving the box around, it couldn't help but swing. For the life of me, I couldn't tell that it swung any differently next to the oil than it did when he walked across the yard.

I pulled a silver dollar from my pocket—in those days you could get a real one just by going to the bank and trading paper for metal, and this was a 1900 Barber in almost new condition—and held it up. "I was to pitch this thing in the dirt and cover it over, you reckon you could find it if you didn't see where I put it?"

"Sure," he said. "I'll turn my back an' you go drop it. Kinda make a circle in the dirt, though, so I don't have to spend all day huntin' it."

I went over to a big liveoak, sketched a rough circle about eight feet across with the toe of my boot, dropped the coin, and kicked a rusty tin can over it. He baited the machine with a flying eagle quarter, warmed it up, and began to search my circle. After about twenty minutes he turned to me.

"You sure it's in this circle?"

"Yep" I said, and flipped over the tin can. The shiny coin, its

1900 date clear in the afternoon sun, lay exposed.

"No wonder," he said. "'At tin can was messin' up the machine. I kept gettin' a pull round there, but it never would come in like it's s'posed to."

I was still unconvinced. "How far down will it go?" I asked. "Suppose that dollar'd been two–three feet deep. Would it find it?"

"Lord, no," he said. "The deeper it is, the more of it gotta be there. 'At gold by the windmill, 'at's maybe eight–ten foot down. Big old box. Maybe two–three hunnert pound. 'At silver ore, now, there's a powerful lot a that, but it's maybe twenny–thirty foot deep. 'Em oil pools, they real deep—couple hunnert foot, anyway. You go huntin' stuff 'at's real deep er kinda small, you gotta have 'nother kinda machine." He shut off the doodlebug and got a small cardboard carton out of the glove box of his battered, prewar Chevy sedan. He opened the box reverently, like a man displaying fine jewelry. From it he took a thin, bright-plated device that consisted of a piece of spring wire about 18 inches long and what appeared to be a long, round-nosed, chrome-jacketed rifle bullet of about .40 caliber. The bottom 6 inches of the spring was a coil, followed by a straight section about 9 inches long, another 1½-inch coil, and 1½ inches more of straight spring that was fastened to the bullet on a swivel arrangement.

"This here's a mind machine," he said. "Works on yer mind. Don't need no batteries er nothin'. Bought it through the mail from a feller in Utah two years ago. Give twelve bucks for it. Grab hold on to the bottom coil here, an' when you get close to silver or gold she commences to spin—like this." He moved his hand and the device began to whirl. "I was up to Burnet this past spring, up on a place b'longs to some of my wife's kin, an' I was huntin' 'at Jim Bowie silver. I hit one place up in some big red rocks an' she commenced to spinnin' like this." He whirled the device until the bullet was level with the ground and made

a whispering, silvery blur as it went past. "Course, I'm makin'
it do that, but I wasn't doin' nothin' to it then. I reckon I was
might near on top of 'at Jim Bowie silver, but I didn't have no
help an' I can't dig out them big granite rocks all by myself."

Nobody, to my knowledge, has ever suggested that Jim
Bowie or anyone else ever found any silver east of the Colorado
River, and Burnet County is entirely east of the Colorado. I
never did dig for that "big old box of gold" next to my neighbor's
windmill, nor for the silver ore in the pasture. Oil there may be,
but not at two hundred feet. It's a pity the doodlebuggers are
dead now. They show you what a man can make himself believe
if he works at it long enough.

By the time the 1970's rolled around my reputation as a lost
mine and buried treasure nut was firmly established. I was
approached, in Dallas, by a neatly bearded, Italian-suited, pipe-
smoking sort who appeared to be either an insurance man or
an instructor in a college business school. He wanted to know
what I knew about the Lost San Saba Mine. I gave him enough
to get him opened up.

The man certainly knew quite a bit about the San Saba
Mine, but it quickly became obvious that all his lore came from
books—he'd never been on the ground. He'd read a lot of books
I hadn't at that time, though, including von Roemer's *Texas*,
apparently in the original German. He was firmly convinced,
working from von Roemer's description of the "mission ruins,"
that the Spanish government didn't build Mission San Saba.
Trouble was, he didn't credit it to the Jesuits, either. He had
someone else entirely in mind.

"The Mission San Saba," he informed me, "was built an
unbelievably long time ago, on the order of several thousand
years. It was built by white men, all right, and it was considered
holy ground by all Indians. That's why the Comanches wiped
out the Spaniards. It was the home of the White God who had
come so many years before—you know how the Aztecs felt, at

170

first, about Cortés—and promised to come again."

"You're a Mormon," I said.

"By no means. The Mormons are on to something, but they've perverted a perfectly reasonable, natural, explainable phenomenon into a pseudo religion. There's nothing paranormal about this. The people who built that place—and a lot of others—were as human as you and I. Perhaps a little different physiologically, but the races are probably cross-fertile."

A light slowly began to dawn. "What places?" I asked.

"Stonehenge. Nan Madol. The Gate of the Sun at Lake Titicaca. The Nazca Lines in Peru. Places like that."

The chariots of the gods had landed with a thump on the San Saba River. The man was a dyed-in-the-wool von Danikenite who believed the Mission San Saba had been built by people from outer space. His interest was not in San Saba silver, he was only interested in finding silver to finance research into people in silver spacesuits. He knew about the diggings on Silver Creek and wanted to know what I knew about them. I told him what I knew and he left happy, determined to raise funds and buy into the diggings on Silver Creek.

One of the many problems with making lost mines and buried treasures your hobby is the character who crawls out from under a rock and wants to call you brother. After meeting two or three of them, you not only fully understand, but also sympathize with the way the air force feels about flying saucers. Fair warning—if you decide to hunt lost mines and buried treasure, be prepared for anything.